YOUTH LEAGUE
PASSING AND RECEIVING

BY
KEN ANDERSON
and
BRUCE COSLET

With
Jack Clary

The Athletic Institute
North Palm Beach, FL 334

Library of Congress Catalog Card Number 89-80693
ISBN 0-87670-117-9

A Word from the Publisher

This Sports Publication is but one item in a comprehensive list of sports instructional aids, such as video cassettes and 16 mm films, which are made available by The Athletic Institute. This book is part of a master plan which seeks to make the benefits of athletics, physical educational and recreation available to everyone. To obtain a free catalog, please write to the Athletic Institute at the address listed on the copyright page.

The Athletic Institute is a not-for-profit organization devoted to the advancement of athletics, physical education and recreation. The Institute believes that participation in athletics and recreation has benefits of inestimable value to the individual and to the community.

The nature and scope of the many Institute programs are determined by a Professional Advisory Committee, whose members are noted for their outstanding knowledge, experience and ability in the fields of athletics, physical education and recreation.

The Institute believes that through this book the reader will become a better performer, skilled in the fundamentals of this fine event. Knowledge and the practice necessary to mold knowledge into playing ability are the keys to real enjoyment in playing any game or sport.

John D. Riddle
President and Chief Executive Officer
The Athletic Institute

James Hotchkiss
Executive Director
The Athletic Institute

Table of Contents

Acknowledgments

Like any successful pass pattern, this effort came about only with the help and assistance of others.

We want to thank photographer Mike Plunkett for his photography, which illustrates much of what we are trying to teach. We also appreciate the efforts of John Monteleone, the book's producer at Mountain Lion Inc., in Rocky Hill, N.J.; Deborah Crisfield, who helped to edit the book; and Martha Wickenden of Mountain Lion, who coordinated everything.

We also appreciate the Cincinnati Bengals making their practice facility available to us.

We certainly enjoyed working with veteran sports media specialist Jack Clary, who ably assisted us in writing the book and whose knowledge of the technical aspects of football helped us draw up a workable and intelligent outline that resulted in what we believe is a very fine book.

We also got a big kick out of working with two terrific demonstrators—J. J. Coslet and Matt Anderson—who are taking their first steps into the sport and for whom we wish a great learning experience and total enjoyment from a game that has been such a rewarding part of our lives.

Ken Anderson and Bruce Coslet
Cincinnati, Ohio

Foreword

The popularity of the game of football has spread like a prairie fire over the last three decades for one good reason: the forward pass. There is nothing more exciting in football than a long, arching pass soaring downfield into the hands of a receiver running all-out, unless it's that player making a leaping catch while displaying the singular bit of marvelous athleticism that is a key ingredient for any pass receiver.

At the top level of the sport, in the National Football League, passer and receiver are capable of working on special wavelengths, honed by years of experience in high school and college. Their talents are polished by hours of practice together, where they begin to think as one person, and then they go out in a game and perform their special brand of magic.

But with all the excellence in the execution of what has now become a most sophisticated means of offense, there always had to be a beginning. For today's current stars it began when, as young quarterbacks and receivers, they took their first tentative steps to play a game they had seen live or on television or had read about. But these young players knew little of the techniques. All they knew was that some of them wanted to throw the ball and others wanted to catch it.

Watch them perform today, with the great skills they seem to exhibit effortlessly, and these simple beginnings are hard to believe. However, without exception, they were all once young kids, stumbling and bumbling around a bit to get their "football legs" beneath them. They started to learn the rudiments of the game and allowed talents they didn't even know they possessed to come to the fore.

Today, there is another group of future stars going through the same process, some of whom may live in your neighborhood or town or be your schoolmates—best of all, you may be one of them yourself. Or you may be a coach who wants genuinely to help young players develop their skills and learn not only to play the game of football but also to enjoy it forever, regardless of how far their careers may carry them. No matter who you are, all who participate in the game should know at the start that there is much work involved to realize success as a quarterback or receiver.

A quarterback's basic function is to handle the ball, either handing it off on a running play or throwing the forward pass. There is a tremendous amount of technique involved in both plays, but what distinguishes great quarterbacks from ordinary or even good ones is their ability to use the forward pass as an offensive weapon. It not only requires a strong arm but also constant work to develop accuracy, study to learn defenses, and a willingness to work hour after hour to perfect the timing that is so important for the success of any pass offense.

For the receiver, it means first and foremost having the ability to catch the football and do it consistently. It means being able to run all-out in perfect balance or catch the ball while almost stopped and off balance. It means being able to reach for it and hold it when it is sailing above the head or lean down and grab it when it comes below the knees. A receiver should not be someone who worries about being hit, yet he should be able to escape defenders, because of a good measure of speed and quickness—of foot and mind—that results in crisp, accurate pass patterns.

Young players starting out may find all of this a bit mystifying, and even at times somewhat intimidating, but coaches can go a long way in helping to alleviate problems and unfold those mysteries in easy, understandable and fun ways that will allow the young player to begin his development. Neither coach nor player should expect instant perfection—even all-pro players don't and it is one great reason why they work hard day after day in practice, spend hours studying film and still are never satisfied with how well they perform.

Above all else, it is important that both quarterback and receiver—and certainly the coach—should always work to make every technique perfect. And all of this should be a pleasurable experience for the players, with emphasis placed on learning and making a strong effort to improve in every practice and in every game.

We have laid out in this book the means by which we believe all of this will come about, and we have based it on fifty years of cumulative collegiate and professional experience and experience as parents who have young sons active in football. We have deliberately stayed away from making this information too technical or only suitable for those who have played at higher levels. Instead, we have aimed it at the player who believes he can become a fine passer or receiver and wants to learn how that can happen. He may play just one year, or he may use what he learns as a springboard to a career that someday may carry him to the heights reached by Boomer Esiason, Eddie Brown, Tim McGee, Isaac Curtis, and Cris Collinsworth, whom we know very well, or by Joe Montana, Warren Moon, Dan Marion, Bernie Kosar, Jim Kelly, Al Toon, Drew Hill, Mark Clayton, Mickey Shuler, Jerry Rice, and Anthony Carter, whom we watch or coach against during the season. Like young players now starting out, these players dreamed of achieving such heights, and their dreams came true. We hope yours will, too.

Introduction

Youth Sports: Benefits and Responsibilities for the Athlete and Coach

Benefits of Participating in Sports

Sports for children have become so popular that an estimated 20 million American children between the ages of six and sixteen play one or more sports each year. This tremendous interest suggests that parents and children believe that competitive athletics contribute positively to children's development. Such a wholesale endorsement may be misleading, however, unless it is counterbalanced by the sobering statistic that approximately 70 percent of the children drop out of organized sports programs by age fifteen. Many of the children who drop out are the ones who could benefit most from organized sports if directed by competent coaches. Thus, every coach, parent and athlete should answer the questions, "What are the benefits of competitive sports for children?" and "How can I be sure that these benefits are available to all children who participate in youth sports?"

Clearly, sports can have both positive and negative effects on children, but positive results can occur only if coaches and athletes conduct themselves in responsible ways. Although many of the benefits are immediately detectable and of a short-term nature, the most sought-after and important contributions of sports to total development are those that last far beyond the athlete's playing days.

In order for the benefits of sports to be available for all children, they must be identified, valued and included in their practices and games. Following are some of the benefits that are most commonly associated with children's sports participation:

- developing various sports skills
- learning how to cooperate and compete

- developing a sense of achievement, which leads to a positive self image
  - developing an interest in and a desire to continue participation in sports during adulthood
  - developing independence
  - developing social skills
  - learning to understand and express emotion, imagination, and appreciation for what the body can do
  - developing speed, strength, endurance, coordination, flexibility, and agility
  - developing leadership skills
  - learning to make decisions and accept responsibilities

The Role of the Coach in Youth Sports

The coach of young athletes is the single most important adult in all of children's athletics. Other adults, such as officials and administrators, have important responsibilities, too, but no task is as important as that of the coach, who must guide young children physically, socially and emotionally as they grow from childhood through adolescence into adulthood.

The youth sports coach is required to play many roles. Most prominent among these are being a teacher and an instructor of skills, a friend who listens and offers advice, a substitute parent when the athlete's mother or father is not available or accessible, a medical advisor who knows when and when not to administer first aid and emergency care, a disciplinarian who rewards and corrects behavior, and a cheerleader who provides encouragement when everything goes wrong.

The age and development level of the athletes will determine how frequently the coach is asked to assume the various roles. Indeed, coaches may find themselves switching roles minute by minute as the fast-moving, complex nature of a contest calls for different responsibilities. The coach's responsibilities in each of the most common roles are discussed in the following sections.

The Coach As a Teacher

Although all of the coach's responsibilities are important, none is more important than being a good teacher. No matter how adept a coach is in other roles, these successes cannot overcome the harm caused by bad teaching. What then, are the characteristics of a good teacher?

Good teachers know what they are attempting to teach and are able to **select appropriate content** for the various levels of ability of their team members. Good teachers are **well organized,** both for the long-term season and in their daily practice and game plans. Good teacher are also **interested in the progress** of all their team members, including those who are inept and slow-learning. In summary, good teachers must love their athletes and their sport so much that practice sessions and games are joyful experiences for coaches and athletes.

The Coach As a Friend

Children play sports for many reasons, but one of the most frequently cited is that they like to be with friends and make new friends. Often, the most important role of the coach is just being a friend to a child who has none.

Being a friend to a friendless child often requires initiative and extra work for a coach, because such children are often unskilled and may have personality characteristics which make it difficult for other children to like them. Often the attention and affection by a coach is a sufficient stimulus for other team members to become more accepting, too. Regardless of the effort required, the coach must ensure that every child feels accepted as a member of the team.

The coach as a friend must be enthusiastic about sports and the participation of all children. Good friends are motivators who reward players with compliments and positive instruction instead of concentrating on errors. Good friends make children feel good about playing sports.

The Coach As a Substitute Parent

Nearly 50 percent of today's young athletes are likely to live in single-parent families. Whether or not coaches want the role of being a substitute parent, they are likely to acquire it. Even those children who live with both parents are apt to need the advice of their coach occasionally.

One of the most useful functions of the coach as a substitute parent is simply to listen to the child's problems. Frequently, the mere presence of an adult listener who inserts an occasional question to assist the child in clarifying the problem is all that is needed. As a coach, you must be careful not to judge the appropriateness of a parent's actions. In most instances the problems between parents and children are simply misunderstandings about children's desires and responsibilities. Such misunderstandings can usually be resolved by discussion, persuasion and compromise. However, in situations where parental actions are resulting in physical or mental abuse, the coach should contact professional counselors who are equipped to deal with such problems.

The Coach As Medical Advisor

Medical problems should be left to medical personnel who are equipped to deal with them. However, as a coach you are usually the first person at the scene of a youth sports injury and, therefore, are obligated to provide or obtain the necessary first aid. In addition, your judgment is likely to be called upon in situations where an injury has occurred and a decision must be made about whether the athlete should return to practice or competition.

A prudent policy for you is to resist making decisions which others are more qualified to make. You should seek the advice of medical personnel when injuries occur. Encourage your athletes to report aches, pains and injuries that are likely to impede their performance. Despite the emphasis on short-term objectives, your job is to safeguard the health of the athletes so that they are able to participate fully in physical activity well beyond the childhood years.

The Coach As Disciplinarian

One of the most frequently cited values of youth sports is their alleged contribution to the behavior and moral development of athletes. However, there are instances in children's sports where coaches and athletes have behaved in socially unacceptable ways. Obviously, attitudes and behaviors can be affected both positively and negatively in sports.

The first step to being a good disciplinarian is to establish the rules that will govern the athletes' behavior. These rules are more likely to be accepted and followed if the athletes have a voice in identifying them. Secondly, you must administer the rules fairly to all athletes. Desirable behavior must be enforced and undesirable actions must be corrected.

The Coach As a Cheerleader

Young athletes are likely to make numerous mental and physical errors as they attempt to learn specific skills. For that reason, their coaches must be tolerant of mistakes and eager to applaud any actions that represent improvement in performance.

Young athletes respond well to praise that is earned and given sincerely. Conversely, they are not very tolerant of criticism, especially when it occurs in association with a coach's expectations that are beyond their capacities or abilities. You must know your athletes so well that your requests are likely to result in a high ratio of successes to failures. When you choose tasks that are challenging but are likely to be done successfully you are in a position to be a **positive coach.** Positive coaches are likely to have fewer discipline problems than coaches who expect too much and then focus on inappropriate behavior. Being a positive coach is a good way to build the self-esteem that all young athletes need in order to feel successful about their sports participation.

The Role of the Athlete

A successful youth sports experience places demands on athletes as well as coaches. These responsibilites should be stated so that athletes and their parents understand what is expected of them. Some of the most important responsibilities of athletes are as follows:

- treat all teammates and opponents with respect and dignity
- obey all team and league rules
- give undivided attention to instruction of techniques, skills and drills
- always practice and play with a clear mind
- report all injuries to the coach for further medical evaluation
- discourage rule violations by teammates or opponents
- play under emotional control at all times
- avoid aggressive acts of self-destruction
- compliment good performances of teammates and opponents
- return to play when an injury is completely rehabilitated

Summary

Youth sports are designed to provide benefits to both athletes and coaches. However, these benefits cannot be obtained in the absence of clearly defined responsibilities. When both coaches and athletes accept and carry out the responsibilities defined in this introduction, then the benefits of youth sports participation are likely to be realized.

Vern Seefeldt, Ph.D.
Director
Youth Sports Institute
Michigan State University

YOUTH LEAGUE
PASSING AND RECEIVING

SECTION ONE
The Quarterback

I. Developing a Young Quarterback

The primary position on every football team is quarterback, and with teams at all levels of competition now relying more and more on passing as part of their offenses, that position is the key to a team's offensive success.

However, the growing importance of the position brings with it added pressure to perform at a high level. The quarterback must be able to execute all of the various techniques of ball handling and throwing. Young players have a tendency to look only at the glory involved at the position without realizing that the responsibilities that go with playing quarterback are probably more intense than at any other position on the team. This translates to just two things: hard work and more hard work. The young player must learn, develop and polish all of the skills involved in handling and throwing the ball, not to mention the intricate footwork that is used before the ball even leaves his hands on a simple dive play or a long forward pass.

Before we even begin to discuss the technical aspects of the job, both coach and player should understand some of the more important ground rules that should apply in developing good football players, regardless of position. In so doing, both will find the football experience both rewarding and fun.

Coach's Responsibilities

Begin by realizing that, above all, the game must be fun. Certainly, teams play to win, but at early levels of competition the fun aspects, coupled with good, solid teaching and total effort, must take precedence. The greatest disservice a coach could do would be to make outrageous demands or place undue stress on winning over the other experiences, thereby turning a youngster off football. Every coach who becomes involved with first-time players must keep in mind that a young player's experience from these years may forever determine his attitude toward the game.

Nowhere is that more apt than at the quarterback position, where that youngster is the center of attention. Young players go out for quarterback for a variety of reasons, and some are not cut out physically to play the position. But the coach should accept each prospect and work with him to the same degree, until it becomes clear to both coach and player just where he is best suited to play.

When a youngster comes out for his first, organized football experience, he already has some feeling for the game, even though he really does not fully understand all that may be asked of him. But the coach must realize that from the time that new player draws his equipment and comes to his first practice session, what he is taught and how he is taught will be one of two major determinants of how far he progresses. Talent will be the other, but a coach at this level should never place absolute emphasis on talent alone to determine whether a youngster can play.

Patience—The Supreme Virtue

Developing a young quarterback is no easy task, and it may require more patience than a coach ever thought he possessed. If the coach finds he does not have the patience for this task, then rather than spoiling the player's fun, he should step aside or turn over the job to someone else who does. We cannot stress enough the need for patience at this level, and it is particularly important in coaching a quarterback because of the multiple physical tasks that this player must perform. A coach can have all the technical knowledge in the world, but unless he is able to impart it in a pleasant atmosphere where the young players can learn and develop, he is wasting his time and hurting his players.

It is also important at this level that the players like their coach, and the coach should not worry too much about the respect issue. That comes at higher levels. When a child begins to play a sport, he is more liable to get into the spirit of his coach's teaching if he likes his coach. In this regard, however, everything should be natural, not forced. A coach shouldn't go out of his way to get a player to like him, because that may lead to more problems than it solves, but if a coach is himself, then his natural friendliness will come through and be accepted. Not every player will respond the same way, but they will know the coach cares for them and is doing all he can to help them learn the game. Then they will open their minds to his teaching and begin the learning process.

A coach also must realize that he is dealing with children and not with the players he sees on television, who are older, more experienced and more talented. His judgments and his expectations must be realistic; college coaches have often told us that even they must catch themselves on occasion and realize that the young men they are coaching are still developing.

This is not to say that a coach shouldn't expect dedication and commitment. Patience also has its limits, and a coach has every right to reasonably demand production and development in return for all that he has expended in his role. But if players know the coach likes them, they will respond, and the best way to achieve this goal is by building practices so the players have fun while they are learning.

Coaches also must do as much research as possible about the game and the techniques being used. (By reading this far, a coach already is on the right track, and by the end of the book he will have fulfilled much that goes with that requirement!) Many coaches haven't played the game for years and are not up to date on the newer techniques. A new coach should watch a high school or college practice, if possible, and talk to those coaches to get added knowledge. Remember, the young players coming out for the first time are hungry to learn, and they will absorb everything they are taught because of this enthusiasm. So teach them the best and most up-to-date techniques.

There are two other areas to avoid. First, forget the "butchy" aspects of football, where the premium is placed on hit-hit-hit and only players who can crunch people are praised as being "real football players." At this level, players will discover for themselves how much of the game's physical demands they can endure. A coach should not scrimmage his team every day to prove it can play football or assign other brutal tasks to "make his players tougher." Instead, he should teach kids the proper way to play and watch the enjoyment they get from executing a good block, run, catch, or a clean, solid tackle. The spirit of the game demands that approach; the other is abhorrent for children who are just learning how to play.

Secondly, a coach must avoid trying to re-create his own past career or trying to atone for the lost days of a disappointed youth. To live in the past is not only self-serving, but it will harm the players. The coach's motives for getting involved should have the youngsters' best interests at heart—and that is the only reason adults should ever be involved with young people.

Players' Responsibilities

Players, regardless of position, must understand that while football is a game and should be fun, there are also certain responsibilities. One of those is that practice sessions really are work periods, not unlike classroom sessions at school. Coaches are teachers, and their subject is football. They must receive all the attention and respect accorded to a classroom teacher. If a youngster comes out for football for the sole purpose of being with his buddies and goofing around, then he is going to be a problem.

Attitude—having a good one—is the player's responsibility every time he comes to practice or plays a game. He must remember that at all times football is a team game. Quarterbacks, more than any other position, find this hardest to remember. It is a great feeling for a quarterback to throw a long touchdown pass or ring up a series of completions, but at all times he must remember that without the blocking of his offensive line or the skills of his receivers, all those good things wouldn't happen. On the negative side, if a receiver drops a pass the worst reaction a quarterback can have is to show his disgust or disappointment. There may be other times when that same receiver will make a remarkable catch that makes the quarterback look undeservedly good; everything evens out. If a quarterback gets sacked, he cannot chew out his linemen publicly because most likely they are working hard to give him protection. Often, sacks are the result of poor play by the *quarterback,* such as indecision or an improper pass drop, not by the offensive line.

Don't Get Hung Up on Numbers

Quarterbacks and receivers will accumulate their own statistics as a season rolls along, but neither should ever place too much importance on statistics alone. The only statistic that counts is how many wins they can help—note that we said *help*—to produce. It doesn't mean much for a quarterback to complete 60 percent of his passes or for a receiver to catch two dozen passes if the team continues to lose. Players who get hung up on personal statistics are selfish, and in the end they will not do their team much good.

A coach must talk to his players and make them realize that they are dependent upon everyone working together. If a coach has a young, hotshot quarterback who is really impressed with himself (or a player at any other position with an inflated attitude), he must gain control of that situation by calmly trying to impress upon the player the necessity of fitting into a team mode—the team is more important than the individual. If the player does not respond, the coach should find another quarterback—regardless of how good the first player may be. That move in itself may be all it takes to bring the selfish player into line. The team must come first or there will be no team, just a group of individuals playing for themselves. Besides, at this level of competition, it is more important that a young player learn such a value system than be given the impression that he is irreplaceable.

Feelings Are Important, Too

A coach must be careful how he treats any player, including the quarterback. We don't mean coddling them by any means, but a coach should learn just how much criticism each player can take in front of his teammates without having his effectiveness destroyed and how much must be done privately to keep him on track. Either way, no favorites, please, and if the quarterback messes up, then he must hear about it in the same measure as any other player. The quarterback must realize at the start that much will be expected of him, and although he probably will get more blame for his team's failures than he deserves, he will also get more credit for its successes.

Similarly, if a player does not become a starter—regardless of position, but this is especially important for quarterbacks and receivers—the coach has a responsibility to explain why, and then the player must understand the reason and accept it. Coaches know that each player wants to start and play as much as he can, but if he is honest with his team and gives each player an equal opportunity without showing favoritism, then the best eleven players on each unit will start. The players who don't may be disappointed and honestly believe they are better, but they must accept their coach's judgment. They should continue working to improve—perhaps eventually winning a starting role—and always be ready to make a contribution when called upon. Perhaps they may even find that another position is better suited to their talents.

Coaches should realize, however, that at this level of competition, every player on the team should get playing time (players who practice deserve to play as a reward for their efforts), because game experience is important in the development and enjoyment of the game.

Players should be aware, though, that they must have total respect for coaches, teammates and officials. This is an absolute must, and a player should give total attention to these qualities. Respect between player and coach is a two-way street, as we noted earlier in this section. A player must understand that a coach has to make decisions based on experience, performance and ability, not prejudice, and the player must accept this. Respect for teammates builds a good feeling within a team. The quarterback especially, as the team leader, must play close attention to his relations with his teammates. He can't be everyone's friend, and shouldn't even try, but he cannot be part of a clique or show favoritism of his own. Players will look at him as their leader on the field, and he must meet those expectations. Equally as important, players should remember that *officials* are the authority figures in a game, and they cannot be abused verbally or physically. There is no reason *ever* for any player to get involved with an official—during or after a game.

The Game's Physical Aspects

Though quarterbacks and receivers usually do not get involved in the constant physical contact experienced by offensive linemen, running backs and defensive players, there are times when they must involve their bodies, which to some means "toughness." At this level of play, no one really knows how tough a player is, but the mere fact that he comes out for the team means he has at least accepted the fact that he will get hit. Thus, there can be no questioning his courage, because he knows enough about the game to realize that he must endure contact if he wants to play. By making that decision, he has set aside his fears and a coach must be sensitive to that decision and to those feelings. Sadly, too many young players start out with coaches who place too much emphasis on the contact part of football, though the players are anywhere from eleven to sixteen years of age and fighting through the natural fears that touch everyone just learning the game. Realistically, a youngster's "tough-ness" at the early stages of his football career, regardless of position, really isn't that important.

The "contact problem" may be most sensitive, particularly with the parents, when a player is just getting started in football. The parents and the player should understand that he will get banged around a bit, but, as long as the youngsters compete at the same physical and age levels and wear the correct protective equipment, they will not get hurt playing football in any greater proportion than in skateboarding or riding a bicycle.

The same goes for receivers, who often are vulnerable to blind-sided hits from defensive backs and make juicy tackling targets whenever they extend their bodies to catch a pass. Yet, they cannot hesitate to challenge any defender at any part of the field and must put all of those dangers aside to concentrate on catching the ball.

It is most important to build the confidence of a player, regardless of his position, and do nothing that will cause him to question his courage. Then, as the player gets better, the natural fears that accompany the physical aspects of football begin to lessen.

We have been involved in the game at every level, and we never have, nor ever will, question the courage of anyone just starting out. We have young sons involved with the sport, and we have always taken great care to allow them to run on their own gas, not forcing them to emulate what we achieved as collegians or professionals. All we want for them is enjoyment from the game for as long as they wish to play it. We have not rushed them into the sport, nor have we loaded them down with information and techniques. When they were ready to compete at the high school level, we allowed them to become part of their school's program and the coaching that accompanied it, and we abetted that coaching with whatever help they requested from us.

Who Can Play Quarterback

As we noted at the start of this chapter, quarterback is the glamour position on a football team, and there are a lot of youngsters who believe they can do the job. But how are a player and a coach really going to know?

A coach should look for a good athlete, one who is a good runner and who demonstrates that he can throw the ball fairly well. The throwing aspect can be easily seen by how well a prospect grips the football and whether he can throw a tight spiral up to 30 yards.

If a player wants to be a quarterback he can develop his throwing simply by playing catch with his friends or his father or mother and working on the accuracy through constant repetition. In fact, it is important for a youngster not to get discouraged when he begins throwing by worrying about how far the ball will travel. *Arm strength* at this level is secondary to accuracy because most of the pass patterns will be at short and medium distances. Completing the pass is much more important than how far it will go. We have all seen kids get into punt, pass and kick contests because they heave a football 40 or 50 yards without any accuracy. The passing game at this level of football centers around being able to complete passes, and that is what a coach should look for and what a player should strive to achieve.

Using a ball that fits a young player's hand size will help considerably. An eleven- or twelve-year-old will have a tough time gripping or throwing an NFL-sized football. It is better that he establish a proper rhythm and technique with the smaller ball and move to the larger one when his hand size increases, still continuing with the proper throwing techniques.

However, proper throwing, by itself, will not make the perfect quarterback. *Good athletes* who play the position bring with them good feet and the balance that goes with their other skills. *Speed* is not important at any level, but quick reflexes, the ability to move quickly when dropping back to pass, as well as foot agility, when moving to hand off and sprinting to throw the ball, are most important. A quarterback needs some decent speed only if the offense is an option-type attack. Then the emphasis is not on passing, so other factors dealing with good feet in the passing game are minimized.

Then there are *mental skills* to be considered as well. Regardless of the competition level, it is necessary to have a quarterback who is willing to take charge and willing to give instructions, as well as to take them. Sometimes it might even be a youngster who hangs back in most situations but who shows his real leadership skills when playing football because he has confidence in his ability to perform. In other words, put him on a football field, and he becomes a leader; put him in another situation, and he is content to be one of the gang. On the football field, he has a sense of the game and he knows and likes what he is doing, and he can communicate that to others. That is what is needed at quarterback.

Mental Preparation

The art of playing quarterback begins even before the kickoff. It begins with the quarterback applying all of his mental and physical talents while always working within the spirit of the team, by being totally prepared to play at the best level, and by setting an example for other players who look to him for performance.

Since most quarterbacks have a good passing arm and adequate athletic skills, the route to success lies in a sound mental approach to the game, even at this early level of competition. He must be able to think under pressure situations and function without error when the defense is doing everything it can to disrupt him. He must be able to focus on his own talents and yet still be part of a team. In short, he must be willing to involve ten other players in the offense.

This comes under the category of being a "smart quarterback," such as knowing which receivers can be relied upon in tight situations and knowing who on the defense is vulnerable when it comes time to make a big play. This all should come together during a quarterback's preparation time, so when pressure situations arise he will not be taken by surprise and will know what he must do.

The mental aspects of the game are lessened somewhat at this level because the game is played in rather elementary terms. However, a quarterback must be able to memorize all of the players, know where his receivers will be on various pass patterns, and be able to recognize and react against whatever defenses he will see. Since it is better to have a modest offense—perhaps five or six running plays and five or six pass patterns—much of the mental part of the game can be sharpened in practice by constant repetition.

At the same time, young quarterbacks should never be given a game plan with which they do not feel comfortable. There is enough pressure on them just learning the game without jeopardizing their confidence even before a game begins. A coach should listen to his quarterback, who should make his own observations about what he can—and cannot—perform. On the other hand, quarterbacks also have the responsibility to prepare themselves fully, and with a limited offense at this level, there really never is any excuse either for coach or quarterback not to be in agreement. If a quarterback cannot throw a certain type of pass, don't make him...or get a quarterback who can.

But once the coach and quarterback agree on what will be used, then the quarterback must memorize it, a tough mental exercise because he must remember not only the plays but also the formations that go with them and when they can be most effectively used. Every quarterback may develop his own system for this mental exercise, but Ken Anderson always found it best to visualize all of the situations in which he would use a particular play—and he could do this without ever going on the field.

New quarterbacks can do the same thing. Start with the first down plays and set up hypothetical situations in which they will be used. Then match them to the kinds of defensive coverages that can be expected to occur. Do it from every spot on the field, and visualize what it may look like in the game. Move to second down situations...second-and-seven...second-and-four...even second-and-more-than-ten. Do this with every play and the situations in which they will be used.

In other words, a quarterback should play the game before the game is played. He should do it with the entire game plan so when the real situations arise he will have "a preview of coming attractions." This way the quarterback will know precisely where to find his receivers and will save precious seconds during a play.

One final thought should be addressed. Young quarterbacks have often said to us that it is almost more than they can do to concentrate on the mental and physical aspects of football preparation and still find time to pursue their studies and other outside interests, not to mention getting sufficient rest and relaxation. We have all gone through that, and looking back at our experiences, there is no doubt that if you find this happening, you should put football in the proper perspective by making it only a *part* of your life and allowing your mind to remain open to other interests. When it comes time to play football, it will be more pleasurable and satisfying.

II. Starting the Play

A pass offense is nothing but a bunch of X's and O's until the quarterback starts the play. And before he can do that, he must be very precise and disciplined in calling the play, taking the center's snap and getting back to the pocket. Failure to do any of those three tasks correctly means that those X's and O's won't help at all.

Since the quarterback is in charge of the offense on the field, his first command post begins in the huddle where he must call the play. Now, many people think this is a very simple matter of just saying a few words and numbers and sending the players toward the line of scrimmage.

In reality, one of the chief causes for breaking down at the line occurs because of faulty work in that huddle, whether by the quarterback or other players. Sometimes a quarterback will mumble the play call so that only some of the players will hear. That's when the guesswork as to snap count and assignment begins—and when seeds for breakdowns are planted.

Make no mistake, the successful use of the huddle is up to the quarterback. His voice must be heard and it must be clear and carry to all the other players. He must keep his head up, face the players across from him, and speak with confidence and authority. He must make them believe that he has confidence in the play by the way he calls it in the huddle. If that doesn't come through, how can he expect the others to believe it will work? He must speak distinctly and not allow his words to run together. Players often botch up assignments or run wrong patterns because they think the quarterback said something other than what he called.

This is the best way to do it. First the quarterback should call the snap count twice ("This is from up on two...This is from up on two"), because it tells the players when the ball will be snapped. Then he calls the play ("Split right, 90 double quick out from up on two"). He has given the pass play and again repeated the count on which the ball will be snapped.

Coaches should work on play-calling in the huddle at every practice, and they should be a part of the huddle so that they know the quarterback is giving his commands in the proper way. One of the best times is after stretching exercises at the start of practice by having the team run a "pep drill" in which the offense runs its plays at a quick tempo. The quarterback should call the play in the huddle and then let the team break to the line of scrimmage, line up and go from there. The same process should be repeated during the eleven-on-eleven phase of practice when the offense is rehearsing its plays against the defense. Calling a play properly is as much a part of practicing as teaching the individual assignments to the players, and if it is done correctly in practice enough times, it also will be done correctly in games.

While the intent of these exercises is to polish unit execution, it also drills into each player the discipline that must be part of the huddle. Discipline in the huddle means the quarterback is the only player who talks. If a player wants to communicate something to him, he must do it between plays, before the huddle is formed, or on the bench. There should be no debating, no griping or no politicking for a particular play once the quarterback steps into the huddle, and if there is, then the quarterback must silence the players and take total command.

At the Line of Scrimmage

Regardless of whether the play is a run or a pass, the quarterback is a busy person once he gets to the line of scrimmage. As he approaches the line, he should first check the defensive alignment, particularly if he has called a pass, because in some rare instances the defense may leave a wide receiver uncovered. All the quarterback wants to do then is to get the ball snapped as quickly as possible and fire it out to him.

Ken Anderson is fond of recalling a game between the Bengals and the Pittsburgh Steelers when one of Cincinnati's backup quarterbacks lined up at Pittsburgh's five-yard line, checked the defense but did not pick up the failure of the Steelers' defense to cover wide receiver Isaac Curtis. Once the ball was snapped, Curtis, without a defender within fifteen yards of him, waved and yelled for the ball, but the quarterback never looked. Instead of scoring the easiest touchdown in the world, the Bengals eventually settled for a field goal.

The lesson there, of course, is to really see something when looking right and left. It may not always be an uncovered wide receiver, but it could be something in the pre-snap defensive alignment that makes passing decisions much easier.

There's a note of caution, however. Many quarterbacks, knowing where the play is going, often give that area of the defense more attention, which can tip off the defense. Instead, survey the entire defense, and the play area will come into view as the scanning occurs. Don't stop there, either, but make a mental note of what is happening and continue the scanning process.

If the quarterback does see the defense in good position to stymie his play, then he can call an audible if he has one and check off to another play. He also should look to see if a cornerback is playing extremely loose, or well back from the line of scrimmage, for other clues as to what the defense might do at the snap of the ball that will make snap decisions much easier in the short span of time he has to deliver the ball.

The quarterback also should check his own team's alignment to see that the backs are in the right position, that his receivers are where they should be, that there are seven men at the line of scrimmage, and that the players are at least one yard behind it.

Ken Anderson often laughs at himself when he recalls a game in which he took his position at the line of scrimmage and believed he saw one offensive lineman lined up offsides. He went to tell him that he was beyond the ball only to sheepishly discover that he had taken a position for the snap of the ball behind one of his guards, not his center, who by the rules, is allowed to extend his body farther than the other linemen. This bit of confusion happens at every level of competition—and it has happened to all of the great quarterbacks!

Once the quarterback has reached the line of scrimmage, he must position himself properly behind the center. His stance depends on the size of his center. A short center will not bring the ball up as far as a taller center, so the quarterback's hands must be placed farther beneath him. If the center is tall, the hands need not go so deeply, so the quarterback won't have to bend his knees as much, and he'll be in a more upright position. From there, he should set himself in the following manner:

- Feet should be parallel, at shoulder width and evenly balanced.
- Knees and back should be somewhat straight so the quarterback can watch the defense while calling signals.
- Right hand (left for left-handed throwers) should be firmly set against the natural curvature of the center's butt, with the other hand below it, the two forming a V. But if the center snaps the ball straight back without rotating it—most will rotate it a quarter turn so the laces wind up in the primary hand—then the quarterback can place both hands together in that natural curvature. Either way, the hand pressure must be firm enough so the center knows precisely where he must place the ball.
- Finger spread is not a worry because the ball comes up endwise and it's easy to grab. But the quarterback must fully concentrate on securing it in his hands, and the center cannot release his hands from the ball until he feels the quarterback take it.
- Hand position is important and there is a precise sequence of actions that must be followed:

FIGURE 2-1

BEFORE THE SNAP: *Before hunkering down to take the snap, Matt stands calmly with his hand resting on the center's back and surveys the defense, being careful not to stare too intently at the place where the play will go (2-1).*

1. Place the hands so that the thumbs are together; then slide the left thumb downward a bit, to form a natural groove for the ball.

2. Keep the pressure of the upper hand firmly on the center's butt so that he has an aiming point. If not, the ball can split the quarterback's hands and wind up either in his stomach or on the ground.

3. When the center snaps the ball it will hit something solid—the quarterback's hands, first the top one, and then the bottom one. The center releases the ball the instant the quarterback's bottom hand comes up and secures it. If it hits the bottom hand first, then he can't secure it, and it may pop loose.

Ball exchanges are simple things to execute, but at every level of play, in almost every game, there seems to be a fumbled snap. The blame lies first with the center for releasing the ball too quickly and then with the quarterback for not securing it properly before drawing away from center.

FIGURE 2-2

PREPARING TO TAKE THE SNAP: *With a tall center, Matt's knees are only slightly bent, but his feet are parallel and at shoulder width so he is evenly balanced. (2-2).*

FIGURE 2-3

HAND POSITION FOR SNAP: *Matt's hands under the center show the left hand placed downward a bit, forming a natural groove for the ball. The upper hand has firm pressure on the center's butt and helps to form a natural aiming spot for the center's snap. (2-3).*

The action between quarterback and center is important enough for them to spend time together doing nothing but exchanging the ball. This can be done away from practice and yet certainly should be a part of every practice, with all centers and quarterbacks taking part. This is particularly important for a pass play where the laces should come up into the quarterback's hands so the ball will be ready to grasp in the proper throwing position. The center can set the ball for the precise snap when he reaches the line of scrimmage.

Quarterbacks Must Sound Off

Before the ball exchange takes place, the quarterback calls signals, and he must do so loudly enough to be heard by the farthest player on either side of the ball. Wide receivers generally will be looking toward the line of scrimmage before a play begins so they can better hear the snap count. The quarterback's voice still must be loud enough so that if he turns his head from side to side, the side away from his voice can hear every word or count.

There are two types of snap counts commonly used—the *rhythmic* and *nonrhythmic*. At early stages of competition, the rhythmic makes more sense because the other requires more discipline and experience.

Rhythmic Count

This is always at the same tempo—hut one...hut two...hut three—with the same pause between each sound. Or it can be merely "hut" or "go" or whatever the coach wants to use to get his team going. This balanced cadence gets a team going more quickly with less chance of error, and this is particularly important for young teams or a young quarterback who is trying to establish a cadence and handle all of the other details on a particular play. Another benefit is that all the quarterbacks on the team will use the same cadence and there is no problem when they are substituted into the game. A drawback is the danger that the defense can also pick up on this kind of tempo, and that gives it an edge as to when to get off the ball. One solution is to vary the snap count, not always snapping the ball on the same number.

Nonrhythmic Count

This is used by teams with more experienced players who have learned the discipline of staying still and not moving until the proper count is called. In this one, there is a short pause—or one as long as the quarterback wishes—between each sound or an accelerated sound mixed in with the regular cadence—Hut...(longer pause)...Hut...(longer pause)...Hut-hut...Hut." The defense obviously cannot anticipate or gather any kind of rhythm and must wait until the ball is snapped, giving the offense an advantage. If a team decides to use this occasionally, then the quarterback must be sure to tell the players in the huddle that he will use a nonrhythmic cadence, and he should repeat it before the huddle breaks.

Dropping Back to Pass

The quarterback's feet will make or break the way in which he sets up to pass, and the way he sets up to pass helps to determine how successful his pass offense will work. He should stand behind the center, on the balls of his feet, until he shouts out the signal for the ball to be snapped. At that instant, the weight is shifted onto the left foot (the right one for lefties). When the ball is snapped, he must lift the right foot to begin his backward move. If he uses a parallel stance under center, he can drop his butt a bit when he takes the ball to get him moving backward on that first step.

TAKING THE SNAP AND DROPPING BACK TO PASS: *Ken stands under center awaiting the ball.*

FIGURE 2-4

FIGURE 2-5

TAKING THE SNAP & DROPPING BACK TO PASS (Cont.): *When it is snapped, he lifts his right foot (2-5 & 2-6) and begins his backward move, immediately bringing the ball into his stomach (2-7) to protect it.*

FIGURE 2-7

FIGURE 2-6

He then lifts it into his chest as he begins to move toward the pocket (2-8).

FIGURE 2-8

At the same time, he must take the ball and bring it into his stomach, just as he does before handing off on a running play (which he also will do if he runs a play-action pass). As he turns to drop back, he must bring the ball in front of his chest, holding it with both hands. Quarterbacks who drop back or sprint out with the ball held in a very high position, sometimes around the ear, may find the move very uncomfortable because the arms won't swing naturally, as they do with the ball at chest level. The quarterback can also move more quickly into his drop area with his hands in the lower position. However, some coaches still may prefer the quarterback to drop back with the ball held high. That is a coaching preference.

The key to getting set up is moving to the drop area as quickly as possible. It allows the quarterback more time to survey the defense, find his open receivers, and not be overrun by the pass rush. But the speed of the pass drop is tied into the method he uses, and the *turn-and-move* is best, especially at this level of competition, because it allows the quarterback to set up more quickly.

The technique is to turn half the body—the side opposite the throwing arm—away from the center of the field and sprint back to the spot from where the ball will be thrown. Then the quarterback must square away his body and be prepared to throw the ball. The quarterback sees only half the field as he gets back into the pocket, so once he squares himself away he must check the other half. This isn't as difficult or as time consuming as it may sound, and much depends on the pattern he has called. If it is a deeper pattern, he should read the coverage down the center of the field as he sprints back, primarily looking for areas where he knows the defenders will be. Once he reaches the pocket, he can set up and confirm that coverage and then pick out his receiver. If the pattern is quick, he must check the position of the linebacker on the side where the ball will be thrown as he turns to set up and then pick out the receiver.

III. Types of Pass Drops

A quarterback can do nothing with the ball until he sets up to pass. Where and how he does it will depend on the type of pattern he has called and the excellence of his own mechanics.

We have already noted that the sprint-back or turn-and-move technique is best for quarterbacks at this level, because it is easiest to learn and will get the passer back and in position to throw quicker than the backpedal move made famous by former NFL quarterback Earl Morrall of the Colts and Dolphins and more recently by Dan Fouts of the Chargers.

At this level of competition, or at least until a young quarterback reaches varsity status in the last stages of his high school career, it is probably best for throwers to concentrate on three- and five-step pass drops because of the types of patterns that are most effective from those depths. Coaches must respect a young quarterback's limited arm strength and concentrate more on allowing him to throw from a point where he will be most accurate. He must be able to get back into the pocket, set up as quickly as possible at either the three- or five-step drop areas, and be in balance and ready to throw the ball from either of those depths. Balance is important because it will impact mightily on his accuracy.

All of this doesn't just happen and the quarterback must continue to practice his pass drops away from the field so that he will know exactly how many steps he needs to set up. While he is learning the proper rhythm, he must also concentrate on speed, getting back to those spots as quickly as possible and bouncing into his set-up position—and he can do all of this without ever throwing the ball. This repetition is so important because it will build good habits; the mechanics will stay with him for as long as he plays the position. In like manner, wrong habits also will stick, and they are very hard to break—sometimes so hard that the quarterback will spend more time undoing faulty mechanics than working on skills he needs in order to progress and win a starting position.

Ken Anderson was a sprint-out quarterback in college, but he was drafted by the Bengals because of his great athletic ability. The coaching staff believed that he could become a reliable drop-back passer. But the transition did not come as easily as everyone hoped. For the first two weeks of training camp, he worked with Bill Walsh, then an offensive coach with Cincinnati and later the very successful head coach of the San Francisco 49ers, and he did nothing but walk through the drop-back and set-up process. He did not use a center or a receiver or even a football. But day after day, he went through the very basic drop-back mechanics, first walking to the right position and then gradually building up to an all-out sprint-back mode.

This may seem tedious, but it is a very good way for young quarterbacks to also master the drop-back techniques. They should do it first by walking the requisite number of steps for a three- and five- step drop. Once the quarterback feels comfortable and knows exactly where his set-up point will be, he can trot back to those spots and set up; when he has become comfortable at that speed, then he can go to an all-out sprint and work to make that as smooth as possible.

Three-Step Pass Drop

The three-step pass drop is used for shorter passes, such as "out" and "slant" patterns, which must be thrown in shorter areas and before the defender has a chance to close on the receiver. Speed in setting up here is so important because the pattern's shallow depth

FIGURE 3-1   **FIGURE 3-2**

FIGURE 3-3

FIGURE 3-4
FIGURE 3-5

THREE-STEP PASS DROP: *The three-step drop must be done quickly (3-1—3-4), and it will carry the quarterback back about four yards behind center, where he sets up to throw (3-5). He finishes by stepping up a yard to throw the ball.*

requires the quarterback to get the ball off as quickly as possible, with all of his mechanics in perfect sequence.

The three-step drop will carry the quarterback about four yards behind his center, and he must then step up and throw. His passes from this area will have a much straighter trajectory, so the passer must have clear lanes between his linemen. If he waits too long, the defensive linemen can recover from the initial pass block—usually one that will knock them off balance or put them on the ground (the "cut" technique), and they will have an opportunity to throw up a wall of hands and arms, or worse yet, sack him.

Five-Step Pass Drop

At this level of competition, this is as deep as young quarterbacks should consider setting up to pass. They should not be overly concerned—but still not ignore—the pass rush, but they should mainly concentrate on getting back, setting up and picking out a receiver. Bruce Coslet has selected patterns that fit this depth and which will provide the quarterback with every opportunity for completions. These will appear later in this book.

The five-step drop will take the quarterback six or seven yards behind the center, and he should be ready to throw on the fifth step. This depth will provide young quarterbacks with enough room to use the strength they have in their arms—in later years, arm strength also will be important because the five-step area is where passes such as the ten and twelve yard "out" patterns are thrown, and they must be hummed. If not, they are hanging out there like juicy plums for a defender. With those kinds of passes, and at that depth, the quarterback does not have the luxury of being able to wind up and throw, but for our purposes here, young quarterbacks will have time to get their arms into the ball.

We cannot totally ignore the *seven-step drop* if only to prepare young quarterbacks for a final level they must one day attain to become polished drop-back passers. This is the depth used by most college and professional quarterbacks for the deeper pass patterns—but even with the greater distance to travel to the pocket, set up, and throw the ball, quarterbacks at these levels of competition take no more than three to five seconds from the time they take the snap from center until the ball is winging toward a receiver.

In so doing, the quarterback must stay in control of his body so that his first four steps backward are longer than the last three to get him sufficient depth. The last three can be shorter so that he gets the proper balance that will bring him into the correct throwing position. On the seventh step, he should be able to bounce forward to that position. Stepping forward, even at the five-step depth, is important because the offensive linemen are taught to try to move the outside pass rushers around the quarterback, thus forming the protective pocket from which he can operate. The passer can help his offensive linemen by stepping up and out of the line in which these defenders are being pushed. Often a quarterback sets up and then imperceptibly retreats a yard farther backward, making himself a target to get sacked. This can happen in the five-step drop as well, so a word of caution: once the quarterback hits the limit of depth in his pass drop, his move should be forward as he sets up to deliver the ball.

There is one last hint to remember. In the turn-and-move, or sprint-back technique, if the quarterback is committed to throw to the side away from his vision (his left for right-handed quarterbacks), rather than having his hips perpendicular to the line of scrimmage, he should keep them at a 45-degree angle as he moves because it allows more of his vision to be focused to the left. This is particularly important when throwing the "out" patterns off a five-step drop. In the seven-step drop, quarterbacks will find their hips more perpendicular to the line of scrimmage because their vision widens to the left side of the field on those last three steps.

Other Pass Deliveries

We do not want coaches and quarterbacks at this level to get too caught up in all of the intricacies of the passing game, but there are some plays that will be very effective as part of an overall offensive scheme that can be worked into the three- and five-step pass drops.

Play-Action Passes

If a team has its running game perking, then this type of pass will be most effective because the defense is so conscious of the damage being inflicted by the runners that the linebackers often are willing to bite at the least hint of another run. It is also a good play on short yardage, third down situations where a run seems to be the logical call. In either instance, the linebackers are apt to follow the running back after a fake, and the quarterback will have more room for his receivers. Even if the linebackers don't fully bite, just those couple of seconds of hesitation can be enough to get a receiver behind them and into the open.

The proper technique to make this play work is for the quarterback to make the defense believe he has handed off the ball to a back going into the line, when in fact he has really pulled the ball back as he drops back to set up. A quarterback shouldn't fall into the "lazy

FIGURE 3-6

FIGURE 3-7

FIGURE 3-10

FIVE-STEP PASS DROP: *The quarterback sprints back five comfortable steps, or six or seven yards (3-6–3-10) with his body perpendicular to the line of scrimmage. The final step brings him into position to set up quickly (3-11 & 3-12) and deliver the ball.*

FIGURE 3-8

FIGURE 3-9

FIGURE 3-11

FIGURE 3-12

FIGURE 3-13

PLAY-ACTION PASSING: *Ken moves with the ball as if to hand it off to Matt (3-13), and makes the fake believable by actually placing the ball into his middle (3-14) before drawing it out and dropping back to pass (3-15). Matt carries out the fake by running as if he had the ball.*

man's fake" routine, where he sticks an empty hand into the runner's middle, easily showing that he does not have the ball. This won't fool anyone and is really a waste of time. He should make the move look like a hand-off, meaning *use the ball as a tool in the fake and do it as if there were a running play in progress.* The runner also must keep going as if he had the ball so the fake will be complete and the linebackers will concentrate solely on making a tackle, not on getting back into pass defense responsibilities.

The quarterback must know the point where he will set up to pass. He may start going straight backward but, after making his fake, wind up behind the guard's position. If that is how the play is designed, then that is the point that the line should be protecting, and they will expect him to be there.

There also are other points to remember in using play-action passes:

1. Single setback formations are not ideal for such maneuvers because the defense won't be fooled by such a set up.

FIGURE 3-14

FIGURE 3-15

FIGURE 3-16

FIGURE 3-17

FIGURE 3-20

SPRINT-OUT PASS: *Ken moves to his right and makes the defense believe he will run with the ball (3-16–3-19), before he rotates his hips and moves his shoulder to face his target (3-20 & 3-21) and deliver the ball (3-22).*

FIGURE 3-18   FIGURE 3-19

FIGURE 3-21   FIGURE 3-22

FIGURE 3-23

FIGURE 3-24

FIGURE 3-27

SEMI-SPRINT-OUT PASS: *Ken drops back and then rolls to his right (3-23–3-25), where he sets up to pass (3-26). He must assume a good throwing position to throw the ball as soon as he arrives at his set point (3-27–3-29).*

FIGURE 3-25

FIGURE 3-26

FIGURE 3-28

FIGURE 3-29

2. The play-action pass must work off a specific running play so the defense will be fooled.

3. Play-action passes on long yardage situations don't make sense because the defense knows a run isn't likely to be called, and even if it is, chances are that it will not gain enough yardage for a first down. So the defense will be thinking "pass" all the way. If this is the case, it is better to get that running back into the pattern immediately as a receiver where he can work to get open.

Fake and Sprint Out

This is an offshoot of the play-action pass where a quarterback tries to break the containment tactics of the defensive end or linebacker by getting outside them as quickly as possible, then setting up to throw, throwing on the run, or just taking off and running with the ball. It is a good tactic to use occasionally to get the defense worrying about any of these three options. If the defense fears the quarterback's running and they move up, he can throw over it while still on the move. Here is the proper technique:

1. Take the snap and sprint out, either to a predetermined point where the quarterback will set up and throw or on a designed path that will have him throw the ball on the run. When throwing on the run, his shoulders must be square to the line of scrimmage, he must be in good balance, and he must be able to go either right or left.

2. If he moves to the side where he normally throws the ball, he should throw it in such a way that he can continue running on the same path that the ball is traveling.

3. If he throws away from his natural side, then he must stop, pivot and set up to get the ball off. He should do this by planting the left foot (for righties) and then quickly making a hop-step turn to get the body facing downfield, with his shoulders, hips and legs lined up and facing his target.

Roll-Out Pass

Those motions listed above are equally important when the quarterback uses the roll-out pass. Whether he sprints out or rolls out, he must have his shoulders facing his target. However, on the roll-out, unlike the other passes, there is no faking, so it is normally a committed move from the snap of the ball. The key to completing the pass is that the quarterback should be able to throw and continue to run on the same path the ball takes to the receiver. That is why shoulder position is so important. A quarterback cannot run to his right, parallel to the line of scrimmage, and throw across his body because he won't get anything on the ball. Even though his legs are carrying him in that direction, he still must rotate his hips and move his shoulders toward the target. If he is a right-handed thrower running to the left, he must open his hips more to get his right shoulder in position to face the target.

There's one final word about throwing on the run. *The quarterback should not try to lead the receiver with the ball.* Instead, he should throw the ball at his body because both passer and receiver are moving at the same pace and the passer's body momentum will naturally take the ball in front of him. If instead the passer tries to lead the receiver, the receiver will never catch up with the ball. Also, the quarterback must follow through just as he does when throwing from the pocket to prevent the ball from sailing over the receiver's head.

IV. How to Throw the Football

Let's make it simple at the start: a young quarterback cannot throw the football if it does not fit his hand.

So the first thing a coach should provide is a suitably sized football for young quarterbacks at the youth league levels so, as we noted earlier, the youngster will be comfortable right from the start and will learn the proper throwing motion. Otherwise, he will be compensating for a ball that does not fit his hand, and when he finally figures out a way to throw it, it will certainly not be the correct way.

When it is done correctly, throwing the football is an action that encompasses the coordination of the hand, shoulders, elbow, arm, hips and feet, all working together in a marvelous symmetry that the quarterback really isn't aware of and one that produces automatic weight transfer from one part of the body to another as part of the throwing motion. Ken Anderson said he never paid much attention to his throwing motion. It had been so automatic for such a long period of time that it wasn't until he was just about finishing his career when curiosity got the better of him and he had his throwing motion videotaped at close range. He broke down all of the actions to see just what happened with that process and was amazed at all that occurred in such a split second.

Getting the Ball into Position

As we noted earlier, the ball should be carried with both hands as the quarterback leaves the center and drops back into the pocket. Once he pops into the spot from where he will throw, the ball then should be pushed backward with the left hand (for right-handed throwers, opposite for lefties) in a motion that will raise it upward and into a position behind the head where it can be cocked and be ready to be released.

Here, the grip becomes very important, and it is safe to say that every quarterback will establish his own particular way of gripping the ball. There is nothing wrong with that, and coaches should allow the player to grip the ball in a way that is most comfortable for him and allows him to throw the ball with accuracy and a tight spiral.

FIGURE 4-1   FIGURE 4-2

There are twenty-eight starting quarterbacks in the NFL, and probably none of them grips the ball precisely the same way. Terry Bradshaw, the Hall of Fame quarterback who led Pittsburgh to the Super Bowl, used to keep the index finger of his throwing hand on the rear tip of the ball before he threw it; other passers have their hands near the middle of the ball. Ken Anderson used to grasp the ball by placing his little finger and the index finger on the laces, with the middle finger and the index finger ahead of the laces and on the seams. His thumb acted as a support beneath the ball; always keep in mind that this is the most important digit—without it, the quarterback cannot grip the ball.

The determining factor will be hand size, and here, we will again note that this is relative to age and physical development. As a boy gets older, his hand is likely to grow until he will be able to comfortably grip a regulation sized football. If that doesn't happen, then he must look for a new position.

But the bigger the hand, the closer to the center of the ball the quarterback may wish to place it—and this goes for the youth league sized football, as well. The important thing is to have at least one finger on the laces. Quarterbacks should not keep a death grip of the ball, either, but rather more of a fingertip grip that keeps it from resting in the palm of the hand. If the ball rests on the palm, there is a

FIGURE 4-3

FIGURE 4-4

FIGURE 4-5

GETTING BALL INTO THROWING POSITION: *Matt and Ken get the ball into throwing position, gripping it with both hands (4-1) and bringing it into their middle (4-2), before carrying it chest high (4-3) back into the pocket. They get into a good throwing posture (4-4), and then push the ball up into position with the left hand (4-5).*

FIGURE 4-6

GRIPPING THE BALL: *The bigger the quarterback's hand, the closer to the center of the ball he should place it. Noted Ken's larger hand (4-6) is closer to the middle than Matt's smaller hand (4-7).*

FIGURE 4-7

FIGURE 4-8

BALL'S POSITION IN THE HAND:
*the ball should be gripped by the
fingertips and not rest in the palm
of the hand (4-8) to produce a
good overhand spiral.*

tendency to throw with more of a sidearm motion because the ball
must come off the palm rather than roll off the fingers, lessening the
quarterback's tendency to spiral the ball or get the proper follow-
through. Throwing the ball off the fingers allows for a pure overhand
motion, a proper follow-through and subsequently the good spiral
that is so necessary for keeping the ball in the air a minimum amount
of time.

Throwing the Ball

There is a six-step sequence, and it is laid out here for right-
handed throwers. Left-handed passers should apply the opposite
side of their body. Here is what a quarterback should do:

1. Grip the ball properly.
2. Push the ball into the throwing position.
3. The weight then is totally on the right side, resting on the right,
or rear leg, which should be firmly planted.
4. The weight transfer, which provides power for the throw, begins
with the left leg lifted slightly, and the left arm moving toward the
target. This opens up the left hip, which is so important for accuracy
because the passer must face the person to whom he is throwing.

FIGURE 4-9

FIGURE 4-10

FIGURE 4-13

THROWING THE BALL: *Ken has the ball gripped properly and pushes it into position behind his head while his weight rests on his firmly planted right leg (4-9). The weight is then transferred as he lifts his left leg slightly and his left arm begins to move toward the target, with the ball cocked behind the head (4-10–4-12.) As the right elbow leads the way with the forward arm motion, the ball is released just past the head (4-13 & 4-14) and snaps the wrist, propelling the throwing arm in a straight-down, follow-through motion that comes across the body (4-15).*

FIGURE 4-11

FIGURE 4-12

FIGURE 4-14

FIGURE 4-15

5. As the ball is cocked to be thrown, the right elbow will lead the way as the forward arm motion begins with the right wrist firmly locked.

6. The weight transfer will be completed with the left foot on the ground as the right wrist and forearm catch up with the hips and the ball is released just past the head.

Don't Forget to Follow Through

Any object thrown with the use of an arm demands a proper follow-through to achieve accuracy. With the football, it is achieved by continuing the throwing arm straight downward. The momentum from its swing will bring the arm across the body in a very natural motion. Don't make this a conscious motion because that can only interrupt the natural flow. But almost imperceptible in the natural rhythm is the action of the wrist, which actually leads the way and is turned, or snapped, by the ball as it is released. This gives the ball a tight spiral motion, helps to propel the arm on its downward course, and brings the body into a squared-up position that is lined up with the path of the ball and the receiver.

Study the stop-action film of a quarterback throwing a football as has just been outlined. It is much like a pitcher throwing a baseball, and every pitching coach never fails to stress the necessity of having a proper follow-through once the ball has been delivered so the pitcher will achieve accuracy and land in a squared-up position.

There is one last point in throwing the ball, particularly for older quarterbacks who are capable of getting the ball in low or who can put "air" under it for longer throws. If the ball is to be thrown low, it should be released a fraction of a second later than the ball that needs more "air" or arc to cover a greater distance. That timing will take care of the nose of the ball, a kind of propeller that takes it from the release point toward the receiver.

Young quarterbacks just starting out, though, should not be as concerned at the start with timing. They should focus on just completing the pass and learning how to lead the receiver when he runs his pattern. We are not going to deal with the timing patterns when the quarterbacks are just beginning to learn the skills of the position. It is only important that the ball gets there and that the kid completes it. A coach should just have him throw to where the receiver is and not get too fancy. Then the quarterback can work on leading the receiver and get a sense of confidence so that he can begin to complete passes using that technique. As he gets older and more experienced, he can widen his techniques to altering his release time for low throws and for deep ones.

SECTION TWO
The Receivers

V. What It Takes

The second part of the aerial connection is the pass receiver, and all the intricacies of running a good passing attack as a quarterback must be complemented by the receiver. In short, a quarterback can have the greatest mechanics in the world, can be accurate, have a strong arm and read defenses as if they were an open book, but unless he has pass receivers who can catch the ball, run those patterns and react to what the defenses are doing, then all of his talents won't really mean too much.

We said earlier that not everyone can be a quarterback, particularly one who is charged with running an attack that will depend on passing, and we say here that not everyone can be a wide receiver, where the responsibilities for carrying out those passing schemes are equally important. Again, the beginning level of competition is a good way to find out whether or not a young player can be a receiver, and if a kid wants to give it a shot, then let him. Both he and his coach will discover in good time just how capable he is of handling the position, and it is just as important for a youngster to have that chance as it is for him to succeed. There are a lot of receivers who make it to pro football who were allowed to prove their talent in the position in youth league even though their coaches might have seen them as prospects in another area.

How does a coach or player know his capabilities at this position?

There are six areas in which all receivers can measure their talents, and contrary to what many believe, *speed* is not the most important. That probably will give hope to many young prospects who realize they are never going to be world-class speed burners, or even come close to it, but who do know they can catch a ball and feel very comfortable doing it.

Now, we're not saying that a tortoise can be a receiver, because the ability to catch a ball is vitally dependent upon how much space the receiver can put between himself and the defender, so there must be some speed involved. Yet, on the Bengals, Cris Collinsworth has been a thousand-yard receiver for many of his seasons in the NFL, although he certainly never could match Tim McGee's speed on the outside, even when he was a much younger player. Cris's old roommate, Steve Krieder, was another who did not possess blazing speed, yet he was one of our most dependable third down receivers because he always had at least enough speed to get open and enough other talents to make covering him a difficult task for a defender.

So again, the question is, what does it take?

First and foremost, *quickness* is needed. A player can get by without speed, but he cannot survive without quickness. Collinsworth's great ability to get open began at the line of scrimmage where he quickly got into a pattern and then did everything with enough quickness that a defender was always a step or two behind him. Included in quickness is the ability to change direction, and here we also are talking about *athletic ability* and *quick feet*. At any level of competition, quickness will provide the necessary separation to catch the ball.

The only time that pure speed can be a factor is when a gifted sprinter, who is a receiver, runs down the field as fast as he can and flies past a defender who may have misjudged his speed or who was out of position to get into coverage. That will work as long as there is enough room down the field and his defensive opposition cannot match his speed over a long distance. Now, if the defender is playing deep enough when the play begins so that he will never allow the sprinter to get past him, then the speed aspect is defeated and it becomes jump ball when the pass comes down. Of course, if that sprinter-receiver also has quickness, then he could make a move that would separate him from the defender and get open to catch a pass with much less trouble. He could, in fact, become an awesome weapon at high school and college levels where there is not the overall pure speed in secondaries to match his own. In pro football, we have defensive backs who run 4.2- to 4.4-second 40's and defensive coordinators who come up with schemes to neutralize a receiver's pure speed and force him to rely on other talents.

There was a time about twenty years ago when pro football went after Olympic sprint champions—the so-called "fastest men in the world"—to play wide receiver, believing they could blaze through a secondary and become awesome offensive weapons. We had one on the Bengals, Tommie Smith, who won a gold medal at the 1968 Olympics, and at the time held thirteen world records. He gave it a solid try but had only mixed results because he had not played much football and thus hadn't mastered some of the other physical receiving skills, namely how to change pace and direction while on the move. About the only Olympic sprint champion of that era who ever became a game-breaker was Bob Hayes of the Dallas Cowboys, the 1964 100-meter Olympic titlist. But Bob was also a college football player and he was well rounded in all of the game's mechanics.

That is not to say that *speed* is not an essential quality, because receivers, after they catch the ball, should be able to outrun defenders for some distance. They also must have enough speed that they will force defenders to back up in fear of being beaten deep—an asset in getting separation—and they must have an ability at times to go deep and get open. Otherwise, a defensive back is simply going to "squat" on a slow receiver and never worry about getting burned by a big play, and that receiver will find it very difficult to get any space to catch the ball. Quarterbacks don't look in the direction of receivers who are continually covered.

So speed is a relative thing—it is great to have outstanding speed as long as it can be integrated with the other prime ingredients that comprise the skills needed to be a good receiver. It is also acceptable, particularly at this level of play, to have less than blazing speed and still succeed, as long as the other attributes are there.

The second most important asset is *good hands*. Much is said about "soft hands" being the hallmark of all great receivers, and that is a physical asset that becomes very apparent when you shake hands with them. You can feel the softness in their hands while also feeling the strength that always played a part in their ability to catch a ball. "Soft hands" gives a receiver the ability to literally absorb the ball when it hits his hands. The "hard hands" guys will try to snatch the ball out of the air and have no feel for catching it when it hits their hands. If they play with a quarterback who throws a hard pass, the problem is worse.

Not every receiver is blessed with totally soft hands, nor are many running backs, who also must catch the ball. Yet, these backs can develop catching skills through practice, particularly if they have good hand-eye coordination to go along with fairly good hands—and all backs must have some degree of hand agility to handle the ball so often without mishap. Pete Johnson was a giant-sized fullback on the Bengals several years ago, who had played at Ohio State where the fullback never saw a forward pass. Yet, Pete, who was a punishing runner for several seasons, including our 1981 AFC title year, learned to catch the ball with some consistency—and in this instance, it was mainly swinging out of the backfield and catching Ken Anderson's flare passes while running over smaller defenders who had to take him on man-to-man. That play was an integral part of our passing game, and Johnson had to learn a skill that was all but foreign to him when he came into pro football.

Learning a skill is one thing, but mastering it to the point of consistency is even more important—and every wide receiver must have a high level of consistency whenever he has an opportunity to catch the ball. This is *mental concentration*, another asset that should be part of the receiver's personal package. Nothing galls a coach more than to see receivers drop balls they should catch, and in nearly every instance, the drop is caused by a lack of concentration.

Often a receiver, particularly young ones who are anxious to make every play a big one, will think about their appearance before they think about catching the ball and putting it away. Later in the book we'll discuss the mental process that should take place whenever the ball is coming toward a receiver, but in short, he must have a mental discipline to block out everything—*and everyone*—around him to concentrate on seeing that ball into his hands and securing it. All the great receivers in pro football can do that, and it's not easy. Consider that there are players trying to strip the ball or knock it away or players simply blasting into receivers in the hopes of jarring the ball loose. Those receivers are aware of this when they are about to catch the ball, yet they must have the mental concentration to block it out.

Another aspect of mental concentration is knowing how to run precise pass patterns and adjusting to what the defense is doing to impede the process. This requires some football smarts and enough discipline and concentration to take time to study the game and become good at the mental aspects as well as the physical requirements. Remember, the mind can be conditioned to perform just as the body can be trained to excel, but in both instances it takes commitment and concentration. A player who masters that kind of toughness will not be error prone, and he will have consistency as one of his talents.

Almost hand-in-hand with mental concentration is *courage*, obviously necessary considering the misfortunes we alluded to that can sometimes befall a receiver as he is about to catch a ball. A pass receiver who is looking for the splash and glory of making the big play should remember that football is first and foremost a physical game, and there is a physical toll that he must be willing to assume. It means that he cannot flinch when his pattern takes him across the middle of a defense where players have the same resentment for a different color jersey as they would for an intruder lurking about their home. These are tight areas, and a receiver must know that there will always be defenders close by and that for a good part of the time, he must be willing to fight for the ball or be ready to get popped as soon as it hits his hands. Many times he is off balance and cannot adequately protect himself, so he simply must endure the contact— and make the catch if at all possible.

Courage is an asset that cannot be taught—it can only be reinforced. In the pros, every receiver has it to a pretty high degree, or else he simply doesn't last too long. There is no room on any team for players who only want to go into "safe" areas. Sometimes even being big doesn't help, because a big guy becomes a more inviting target.

One of the great heroic feats during Bruce Coslet's time with the Bengals occurred in a game against Cleveland at Riverfront Stadium. Pat McInally, who was used primarily as our punter but who also had to play wide receiver on this occasion, took a vicious smash after catching a pass, and he was carried off the field. Yet before the game had ended, he returned to catch the winning touchdown pass. Also, on an icy day against the Steelers, again at Riverfront, Pat caught a winning touchdown pass on a bang-bang hookup with Anderson but ended up being absolutely pole-axed by a Pittsburgh defender. Somehow he still managed to hold the ball.

Now, it is only natural for a young player just getting his feet wet to be a bit shy and turn his head when he gets his first taste of contact. But a youngster who has the necessary courage will soon work past that and discover that it really isn't so bad. The more he is exposed to it, the more confidence he will gain so that in a relatively short time—certainly before the end of his first season—he will be all but oblivious to it. That isn't to say there won't be times when it may hurt a bit, but players who have the ability to block out the fears from contact will also have the ability to shrug off the hurts and get right back up and continue to play with the same vigor. It is the same in baseball where a good young hitter gets popped by an errant pitch, and then finds himself ducking away from inside pitches to the point where his hitting begins to suffer. That hitting ability isn't worth too much under those conditions, and in football, a player who can catch the ball really well but who doesn't like to do it in areas of heavy contact will suffer the same fate.

If a young player is shy about contact—at any position—then the coach has to make a determination about his future. Sometimes a coach can simply make it plain to the player that if he wants to play, then he must endure. When the player himself makes the judgment that he'd rather endure the contact than give up the sport, he will naturally gain more confidence. All it takes often is for a player to get hit a couple times and realize that his body still isn't missing any parts, and he is fine thereafter.

A receiver certainly cannot be worried about such matters, and the good ones can come back from getting hit and continue to play with great abandon. Those are the ones every coach wants on his team...those and the ones who have quickness, quick feet, athletic ability, good hands, mental concentration and a fair amount of speed.

VI. Running a Pass Pattern

"Run out for a pass."

That has been one of football's favorite expressions ever since someone discovered that footballs were meant to be thrown. In the early days of football, when it was considered almost less than sporting to do anything other than run between the tackles, the rulemakers not only imposed many obstacles on teams that wanted to throw the ball, but the ball itself was shaped much like an egg and difficult to grasp for any kind of precision passing. In those years receivers primarily ran straight line patterns and waited for the ball to catch up with them.

Not any more. A pass receiver now is a bit of an adventurer because pass offenses look more intricate than road maps. But nothing really happens with these patterns until the receiver gets off the line of scrimmage and begins to penetrate the opposition's defenses.

How to Get Started

Getting started isn't as easy as it may sound if the receiver wants to get a quick jump on the defense and get the advantage for himself.

The two-point stance is preferable to a three-point stance, such as the one a running back assumes, because the first thing a player does in a three-point stance is to stand up into a two-point stance. If the player is there already, then he has saved an extra movement and gotten into his pattern that much quicker. The two-point stance also allows the receiver to see more of the field. He can look straight ahead and to both sides to check the coverage, as well as look in at the ball—when he cannot hear the quarterback's cadence—in order to move off the line the moment he sees it snapped. It also gives a receiver the opportunity to rid himself more quickly of any bump-and-run coverage or a defender rolling up close to the line of scrimmage to cover him.

The first rule is that the receiver should be comfortable in his stance even before the ball is snapped. His body should be leaning slightly forward and the feet can be staggered. At this level of

FIGURE 6-1   **FIGURE 6-2**

THE CORRECT STANCE: *The wide receiver stands at the line of scrimmage with his knees bent slightly, arms hanging comfortably at his sides and 80% of his weight resting on the front foot, and he looks in at the football (6-1 & 6-2). Coach Coslet demonstrates the proper stance with J.J. (6-3), who then practices the technique (6-4 & 6-5). To get started in his pattern, Coach Coslet lifts his front foot, causing his body to move forward (6-6) in a rolling start.*

competition, if a coach uses very simple, straight-ahead patterns, then it really doesn't matter which foot is up and which is back. But if he uses "step patterns" where cuts are made after a certain number of steps and where the outside foot must be up or back depending upon what the receiver will do in a particular pattern, then foot placement is important. We'll look at those mechanics later in this chapter. Either way, with young players just learning the basics, it is better that they first stand comfortably and then work into more intricate maneuvers.

The feet should be shoulder width apart, with most of the weight on the front foot. The receiver must bend the front leg. This helps to create a "rolling start," which means that as soon as the ball is snapped, the receiver lifts his front foot. Instantly, when the weight on that front foot is removed, his body will begin to fall forward, and in a reflex action, he will move the foot forward and put it down again to keep from toppling over. That action really is the first step off the line

FIGURE 6-3

FIGURE 6-4

FIGURE 6-5

FIGURE 6-6

of scrimmage and the one that gets the body moving forward; when the foot comes back down, the receiver can use it to shove off.

So often you see receivers, after the ball is snapped, trying a series of juking moves with their feet at the line of scrimmage, and about all that does is chew up the turf. This won't faze a good defensive back, because he's been taught not to react to a receiver until he sees him move forward. All that action merely delays the receiver and disrupts his timing; chances are the quarterback will go someplace else with the ball. This makes the job much easier for the defensive back because the receiver has taken himself out of the play.

Getting off the line of scrimmage is much like a sprinter coming out of the blocks at the start of a 100-yard dash. Just as a sprinter shoves off on the front block set on the track, so too should a receiver shove off on his front foot—and he should do it as fast as possible. This action must be repeated on every play (yes, even a quarterback sneak) because if a receiver does it only on a pass play, then this just tips off the defense as to whether a run or pass play is under way.

Keep Those Eyes Open

When a receiver comes off the line of scrimmage, his head must be up, and his eyes should start immediately checking the defensive players to see whether the coverage is man-to-man or zone. There are some quick clues, such as the intensity of the defender nearest to him. If he is rushing to get up on him, then the receiver knows he will be getting man coverage. He also can check the three closest defenders—the cornerback, free safety and first inside linebacker—and also see what kind of drops the inside linebackers are taking. Within the first three or four steps, those defenders will tell him what coverage he can expect by the way they move to their coverage areas. If the linebackers turn and move backward on an angle, he can be pretty certain it will be zone; if they stand their ground for a moment or two and look for someone to cover, they are likely going into a man-to-man defense. It is the same with the cornerback and safety. Backs who turn and move to an area are getting into zone coverage; the backs who literally mirror or shadow a receiver are likely to give him man-to-man coverage. But it is up to the receiver to see all of this and recognize what is happening, because the quarterback, looking for the same clues, will react according to what defense he sees. If the receiver misses the coverage while the quarterback reads it correctly, then the chance for a mistake—spell that *interception*—is great.

Pressure That Defender

Once the receiver has come off the line of scrimmage, a turf battle immediately begins. The defensive back considers the territory he must cover to be his own; the receiver is out to grab as much of that as he can for himself. In both cases, the play will be aggressive because the defender will do everything possible to prevent the receiver from catching the ball, and the receiver must do everything he can to see that he gets the ball.

The pass receiver can concede nothing—and that should fracture any notion that being a receiver isn't a tough job. The receiver must be as aggressive, under the rules, as the defender will be under the same rules. This means one thing—pressure the defender, come at him full speed and do it that way on every play. Why? Because if the pattern is run at a leisurely pace where the receiver does not get close to the defender, then that defender has a comfort zone in which he can mirror what the receiver is doing. The key to good defense is the same in football as it is in basketball—go everywhere the offensive player goes and deny him the ball. Therefore, if the defender has been told by his coach not to get beaten outside and deep, the receiver must pressure those areas then run his route. If, instead, the receiver runs inside at this defender, then he will not be pressured, will not worry that he may be going deep, and will just "squat" on the receiver.

So, when the receiver comes off the line of scrimmage, he must close on the defender, pressure him and make him feel uncomfortable. He must intensify that pressure right to the "top of the pattern," or the instant that he "bursts" or makes a move to free himself. This is a move in which the receiver tries to make the defender believe he is going to do something entirely different from what has been called: that he will be going deep, when actually he will be turning inside and coming back to the ball, that he is going to run across the middle when in fact he is going to run an "out" pattern, that he is going to stop and turn around, when he really is running a deep "streak" pattern.

Body Language Is the Key

How does a receiver do this? There are many ways.

A very easy first trick is to look the defender squarely in the eye. That will make him very nervous.

Secondly, the receiver must simulate with his body lean and by running with the sprinter's style—arms pumping, legs bent, body

FIGURE 6-7

CLOSING ON A DEFENDER: *The wide receiver must quickly "close" the distance between himself and the defender, forcing him to backpedal (6-7—6-9). By positioning his body in a sprinter's running form, he makes*

FIGURE 6-9

FIGURE 6-8

the defender believe he is going to run at full speed down the field. The receiver reaches a point where he then bursts to get separation (6-10) from the defender and catches the ball without hindrance (6-11).

FIGURE 6-10

FIGURE 6-11

FIGURE 6-12   **FIGURE 6-13**

THE CUT MUST BE PRECISE: *Coach Coslet demonstrates the proper way to make a cut while running a pass pattern, first by running as fast as possible to close on the defender while also having his body under*

forward to lower his center of gravity for making quick turns—that he is going to run a 100-yard dash while at the same time knowing he may stop at some point at the top of his pattern and burst in another direction. We call this the "burst technique," and it is the most effective way to run a pass route. It is one of the things the Bengals look for when they scout college receivers.

It requires constant practice to perfect this running of pass patterns with a low center of gravity, but it is essential for a receiver to get "down" into his cuts, because he must be able to stop and turn quickly. If the receiver keeps a high center of gravity, he will fall over or be forced to take a couple of extra steps to make a turn. Those extra steps are all that a defensive back needs to get up on him and prevent him from getting open to catch the ball.

As we noted before, the defender is taught to mirror the offensive player so his body lean will be the same as the receiver's. The defender will have his body leaning backward as he backpedals in coverage. The receiver must continue to make his body lean while the defender is backpedaling and then make a sudden move, because the moment the receiver straightens up to stop, the de-

FIGURE 6-14   **FIGURE 6-15**

*control (6-12 & 6-13). He then lowers his center of gravity and begins his
break by turning his shoulder (6-14), and finishes his change of direction
in position to catch the ball (6-15).*

fender will do the same thing and drive on the receiver. If the receiver
has run his pass route aggressively as we have described, he also
has created a space between himself and the defender—a cushion
of yards—that the defensive back must make up. In the time that it
takes him to cover that ground, the receiver should be able to catch
the ball, put it away and begin moving downfield.

Body language really will sell those moves, and this includes not
only the feet and body lean, but also shoulder and hip movement.
When running patterns like hooks (to the inside) or comebacks (to
the outside), where the receiver must stop quickly, turn, and then
come back to the ball, the defender must believe that the receiver is
going to go deep.

If the receiver is running a slant pattern or a post pattern (which
really is a deeper slant pattern) against man-to-man coverage, he
must make the defender believe that he is going to break to the
outside when he really will break to the inside. The receiver can do
that simply by the way he moves his hips and shoulders. If he is
content only to use a head fake and break in, he'll be followed. The
defender isn't going to buy the fake, because a receiver does not

make a really good move with just his head. But if the receiver opens the shoulders and hips as if he is going to the outside, he will have an advantage; the defensive back will bite on that body movement and begin to move outside.

If those patterns are run against a zone defense, the quarterback will look to throw the ball to a "soft" or open spot in the zone, and the receiver must adjust his speed to get to that area at the proper time. But he also must get the defender in the zone looking for him to go in another direction, and again, the movement of hips and shoulders will do the job.

In either case, those body movements must be quick, and they can only be properly achieved by lowering the body and, thus, its center of gravity. If the receiver runs in a high position, he won't have very much body control to make quick turns or abrupt changes of direction.

The feet play such an important role in these movements, particularly for patterns we referred to earlier in this chapter as "step patterns" that require a *plant-and-cut move*. There is a definite sequence for making these moves. For instance, if the receiver is lined up on the right and wants to run a slant pattern, he must plant the right foot on the fifth step to make that cut. But before he even leaves the line of scrimmage, he must be certain that his outside foot is back in his stance so that when he gets to that fifth step, his "plant foot" is properly positioned. There's a good rule of thumb to follow: on a pattern requiring an odd number of steps, the back foot in the stance is the "plant foot"; on one requiring an even number of steps, the front foot does the pivoting.

If the receiver is running a five-step pattern, on the fourth step he makes his move. Then he plants his foot on the fifth step, lowers his center of gravity and gets down on that leg to drive off it as he actually makes his cut. Some people call this the *stick-and-move* technique—stick the foot in the ground and move. Then it is like any athletic move involving balance. If the receiver is going to the left and cutting off the right foot, he wants to stick his foot in the ground and have most of the weight on the inside of his foot. If he gets the weight over the outside of the foot, he may fall over or be well out of balance.

A receiver also can use the "cross-over technique." If he is lined up on the right and wants to run an out pattern, instead of planting his left foot in the ground and cutting right, he can plant the right foot and cross over with the left and "run around a corner." Our receivers on the Bengals, with the exception of Cris Collinsworth, have mastered this move, but Cris is such an excellent "plant-and-cut" receiver that it doesn't lessen his effectiveness, and he is more comfortable doing it that way. And who can argue with his results?

Change of Direction: Measuring Real Football Speed

Wide receivers often are at a "pure speed" disadvantage against defensive backs, but that disadvantage can disappear for one reason: the receiver knows where he is going, and the defensive back does not, meaning that a receiver acts, a defensive back reacts.

So the key to getting open on all patterns that require more than one move is how well a receiver can change direction. If he can get a defensive back moving the wrong way for just a couple of steps, then he can get enough separation to catch the pass. This is where the "burst technique" comes into action and the receiver must use a different kind of speed: real football speed, the kind a receiver must have to get open whenever he changes direction in his pattern.

Some of football's best pass receivers do not have great straight-ahead speed; they are superb in the way they use the speed they have in order to get free to make a catch. It is not how fast they run forward but how fast they change direction—again, their football speed. Cuts must be crisp and sharp. As we noted, a rounded corner on a cut by a receiver can cost enough time to allow the defender to recover.

Separation: The Key to the Passing Game

If the receiver cannot get any separation between himself and the defender covering him, then that defender is going to be there whenever the ball arrives—regardless of what kind of coverage is used—and knock down the ball, or worse, intercept it. That is where the receiver's weapons—burst, faking the deep run, the shoulder and hip movements—are so important; he isn't going to catch many footballs without them.

So although the receiver must be on top of the defender in order to push him, the key is to back off at one point so there will be enough time to catch the ball, tuck it away and begin to move downfield. There must be a feeling between the quarterback and the receiver when this separation is at its best. Anticipation on the quarterback's part is very important because he must have the ball delivered into the receiver's hands at the time when the separation is at its optimum. Since the ball takes so many seconds to travel in the air, depending upon the length of the pattern, he must know the timing of the throw.

That is why, as we noted earlier in the book, quarterbacks use various types of drops in throwing the ball. The longer patterns require deeper drops, the short ones require lesser drops, and thus the ball either has a greater or lesser distance to travel. If for example, the receiver runs a slant pattern and the quarterback takes a five-step drop, he will have made his cut before the quarterback has retreated five steps. By the time the ball is delivered, the defender could close the separation and be able to make a play on the ball. However, if the slant pattern is run and the quarterback instead takes a three-step drop, the ball will be delivered to the receiver before he has made his cut, reducing the time the ball has to travel before the receiver catches it and therefore decreasing the chance of the defender batting it away.

Adjusting on the Move

The receiver also must be capable of adjusting on the move because many times the defense will be in the correct alignment against the pattern that has been called. What happens then? It is up to the receiver to adjust to what is happening as he moves through the pattern.

For instance, if the receiver is running a hook pattern to the inside and there is a linebacker coming from the inside into the area where he planned to hook, does he continue on that planned route? Certainly not. He either must hook well inside of him or adjust and slide to the outside.

Always remember one principal rule: *never run a pattern to get covered; always run a pattern to get open.* We're not saying this is like street football where a receiver runs around and around trying to lose the defender, but the receiver must have a clearly defined set of options based on what the defense does. Taking that information, the receiver—and more importantly, the quarterback—then knows exactly where to move when he finds himself facing the right defensive coverage. There can be no free-lancing in this type of system because both quarterback and receiver must see the same situation and go to the options. They both must be on the "same page" in their thinking. If one decides to do something different, then the opposition may be in prime position to get an interception.

When adjustments are made, the receiver must move to find the best throwing lane, by getting to an open area where he can see the quarterback and the quarterback can see him. The quarterback should anticipate the receiver moving to that open area, and the receiver must make the necessary adjustment every time. If the quarterback anticipates the receiver hooking inside and the linebacker dropping to the outside, he will throw the ball to the inside. If the receiver doesn't make the same adjustment, then the pass will fall incomplete—or worse still, be intercepted.

VII. Catching the Ball and Running with It

The main idea of being a pass receiver is to catch the ball. We are not downgrading the blocking responsibilities, by any means, because any assignment on any play is important, but in football today, the importance of the pass receiver's ability to catch the ball has never been greater. Footballs are flying like never before at every level of competition.

We discussed the importance of having the skill to catch a football, and there are very definite athletic techniques that are a part of this talent. If a player doesn't have them, he should consider another position. There are players who want to become receivers and who seem to have potential in one area but who flame out because they could not master all the techniques and perform on a consistent basis.

A big part of the reason was they simply could not adjust the various parts of their body to catching a football, and a football doesn't always come to a receiver the same way on two consecutive plays. We often hear, "If the ball hits your hands it should be caught," and I don't entirely discard that notion, though there are times when passes hit a receiver's hands and are not caught—and the reasons aren't necessarily the pass catcher's fault.

You Must See It to Catch It

Only receivers and quarterbacks—and probably harried offensive coordinators and receiver coaches—really appreciate the important role that the eyes play in catching a football. Others just see the ball grabbed by the receiver and don't appreciate the mental concentration that is involved in making that catch.

Watch the ball into the hands. Since the first time man ever decided it was as much fun to throw and catch the ball as it was to run with it, coaches have stressed with their receivers that they must "look the ball into their hands." That means they must watch that ball from the time they see it in flight and not even blink until it is tucked and secured in their hands. Some coaches used practice footballs and wrote numbers on them. During drills they would stop and ask the receiver for the number on the ball that he just caught. If the player gave the correct answer because he had watched that ball all the way into his hands, he continued in the drill. If he didn't, he often was seen running around the field doing some laps or worse still, sitting on the bench during the game.

Catch the Black Dot. If the ball passes the receiver's eyes, he will have a hard time catching it, or at best, he will just catch the tail end of it—under most circumstances, not a successful technique. We teach the *"black dot"* method with the Bengals—having our receivers focus on what really looks like a large, black dot as the ball comes toward them. This comes from the tip of the ball where the pieces of leather all come together and form a hole at either end. When the ball is spinning in flight, and the receiver is watching it come toward his hands, all he really sees is that tip looking like a black dot.

A receiver must concentrate on catching that black dot because the whole ball comes with it. The receiver should not concentrate on catching the whole ball because he'll bypass the tip, and therefore the

FIGURE 7-1

CATCH THE BLACK DOT: *The receiver should always concentrate on watching the "black dot" (7-1) which the tip of the football resembles as it sails through the air toward him.*

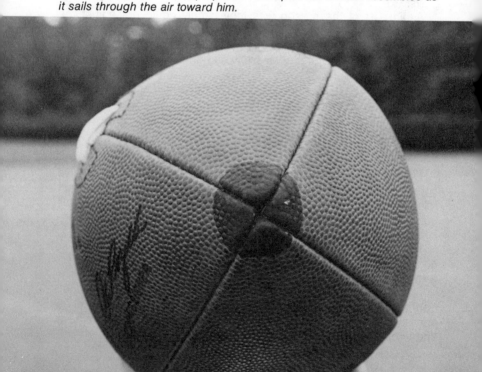

ball will be past his eyes when he tries to catch it. There is a great deal of mental concentration involved here because the receiver must focus on a specific point on the football and not take his eyes from it until he has it secured in his hands. Too often, dropped footballs are a matter of a receiver losing that concentration and looking away from the ball to other action or potential action around him. Once he has watched that ball get into his hands, he must snap his head down on it until he has it in complete control.

Hands...Hands...Hands...

If a running back's legs are his bread and butter, then a receiver's hands are his. That means both hands, because a football should be caught with both hands whenever possible. The one-hand-catch-second-hand-control simply doesn't work too well. Also, too many receivers allow the ball to hit their body and then attempt to control it, and this leads to more dropped passes than completions. Watch the great or natural receivers and they try to catch every pass with both hands; then they bring the ball into their body and secure it. Balls that hit the body first most often hit the area around the shoulder pads, which is hard and unyielding, causing the ball to bounce away before the receiver can control it.

There are times, however, when a ball can be caught within the body's frame, always around the stomach area so the body can help absorb it, but these are limited primarily to short, over-the-middle passes, where the receiver may be directly facing the quarterback and the play is designed to get just a few yards. Running backs and tight ends primarily run these kinds of patterns.

It is the way that a receiver uses both hands that will spell his success or failure. We have seen, played with and coached some of the game's greatest receivers, and all of them had one great asset—they knew how to use their hands in every conceivable situation to catch the ball.

As we noted before, not every pass comes to a receiver the same way, so he must have the ability to shift and change his body to make the difficult catches with as much apparent ease as with balls thrown directly into his hands. This is where hand position is so important.

Any pass that comes to a receiver above his numbers should be caught with the thumbs together. This means the hands are facing toward the quarterback so the ball will hit them squarely in the palms. Try it any other way at that position, such as scooping the ball into the body, and it just doesn't work very well. If the ball comes in the middle of the sternum, the receiver can bend his knees, lowering his body a bit and catching it with his thumbs together. A receiver should be

FIGURE 7-2

LOOK THE BALL INTO THE HANDS: *Coach Colet teaches J.J. that he must focus his eyes on the ball (7-2) and "look it into his hands" (7-3) until it is secured to his body (7-4). J.J. then practices the correct*

FIGURE 7-4

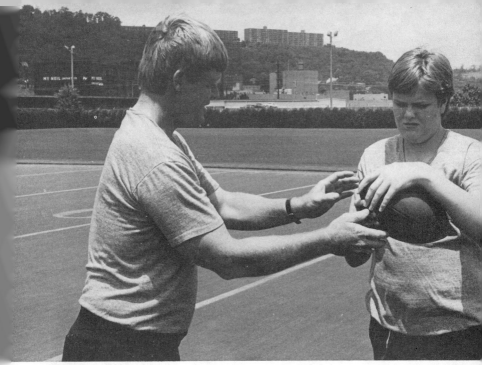

FIGURE 7-3

technique, taking care to snap his head downward to see that the ball is securely in place (7-3–7-8).

FIGURE 7-5

FIGURE 7-6

FIGURE 7-8

FIGURE 7-7

FIGURE 7-9

CATCHING THE HIGH PASS:
When the receiver must catch a high pass, he keeps his thumbs together and turns his hands outward toward the quarterback, taking care to focus on the "black dot" and catch the ball in front of his eyes (7-9).

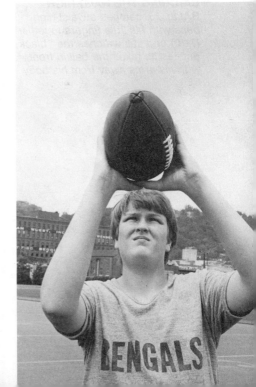

careful about jumping for a ball, because it takes time for the body to come down and regain a running position. He should also avoid raising the body, putting the little fingers together and scooping the ball into the body. It can be done, but a receiver may drop more than he catches.

For balls below the numbers, this can be done. The little fingers are together so the ball can be scooped up into the body. This effects a greater measure of control because a receiver must go down to get the ball, and as a result, he has a greater chance of controlling the ball with that style.

For balls to the side, in front or behind, the receiver should do what is comfortable when he must make an off-balance catch. However, if the receiver uses the little-fingers-together style, the basket that is formed by the hands will not be as strong. Some receivers put their thumbs together and turn their hands in an awkward postion, but balls bounce in, out and off the hands too often. He really must concentrate on absorbing the ball on these types of catches. For instance, on balls thrown *behind the receiver*, the back hip will get in the way of allowing the hands to "give" with the ball; when they hit the hip, the ball will pop out. To remove that obstacle, the receiver must

FIGURE 7-10

***CATCHING THE WAIST-HIGH
BALL:*** *J.J. catches a waist-high
pass with his little fingers together
(7-10) and still watches the "black
dot" as he takes the ball in front
with his arms away from his body.*

FIGURE 7-11

CATCHING THOSE WIDE THROWS: *On a pass thrown to the side, J.J. catches the "black dot" before it passes his eyes, forming a strong "basket" for the ball by keeping his thumbs together (7-11).*

turn his body by pivoting his front foot in the direction he wishes to turn, similar to a pivot move in basketball, and then move the back foot to get the rear hip out of the way. The receiver will be off-balance and out of kilter when he gets hit after making one of those catches, but that is just an uncomfortable part of the job.

For extremely high or low throws, the receiver should forget about making a clean catch. He should first concentrate on just stopping the ball at the "black dot," and if necessary, use a second chance to bring the ball into the body for control. If the receiver at least stops the point, he has a chance to tip the ball to himself.

The receiver should never jump or dive for high or low passes, unless it is absolutely necessary, because he will lose control of his body. Too often catches are muffed or, if made, the chances of getting downfield are diminished. The time involved to regain control allows the defender to get into the play.

If the throw is *high*, the receiver should get his hands over the point of the ball. This will deflect the ball downward and prevent the dangerous tipping action that often turns into an interception. A big mistake many receivers make is jumping unnecessarily for the ball.

FIGURE 7-12

FIGURE 7-13

CATCHING THE HIGH THROWS: On this very high throw, the receiver stops the point of the ball with his fingers on the tip of the ball (7-12), and tips it back to himself (7-13), while keeping his eyes sharply focused on the ball (7-14) and securing it into his body (7-15).

FIGURE 7-14

FIGURE 7-15

FIGURE 7-16

CATCHING THE LOW BALLS: *To catch very low throws, the receiver must bend his knees and form a cradle with his little fingers together (7-16) so the ball can hit them and he is able to "give" with it (7-17).*

FIGURE 7-17

FIGURE 7-18

FIGURE 7-19

Coach Coslet shows J.J. how to form a cradle with his hands, and extend them completely under the ball (7-18). J.J. then gains control of the ball (7-19), and brings it into his chest and secures it (7-20 & 7-21).

FIGURE 7-20

FIGURE 7-21

Again, there is a loss of body control and the opportunity to make a bigger gain.

If the ball is *low*, the receiver should bend his legs to catch it. Many receivers simply try to reach down for the ball. Bending the legs in a squatting position is key because it opens the knees and gets them out of the way, allowing the fingers to get under the point of the ball so the hands can scoop it into the body. If the ball is so low that the receiver must dive for it, he should scoop the ball and at the same time, roll to the ground on his shoulder. This prevents the ground from knocking the ball loose. The receiver should actually overreach for the ball so it will hit his forearms. If he can dive low enough so the ball will hit his arms instead of just his hands, he has a chance to control it on the rebound; if the ball hits the hands only, it may ricochet.

(Body) Position Is Everything

The receiver's body should always be between the ball and the defender, just as in basketball when a good rebounder blocks out under the basket to keep an opponent away from the ball. There will be times when a receiver will have to vary his speed, slowing down or going faster to get his body in position to make a catch.

Much depends on what kind of pattern is being run. If the receiver is running a streak pattern and has to slow down or speed up to catch the ball, he wants to extend his arms if possible and keep the defender behind him so he cannot get to the ball—or if the defender tries, he'll have to go through the receiver first and that means a pass interference penalty. If the receiver is running a hook pattern and the ball arrives a bit late with the defender driving from behind, the receiver must make his body as big as possible. Again, the defender will have to drive through him to get the ball. That takes away his clear path to knock the ball down or intercept it, and it means more completions and yardage for the receiver.

How can a receiver "make his body bigger"?

The receiver can expand his shoulders, lift his arms, widen his elbows or simply raise up and just try to make himself taller and wider. This will prevent the defender from reaching around to swat the ball or, worse yet, running around the receiver to intercept it.

Tucking and Running

The most precious commodity on a football field is the football. Every player who handles the ball during a game must keep in the front of his mind that it is so valuable that it must be protected at all costs.

FIGURE 7-22

FIGURE 7-23

FIGURE 7-24

***PUT THE BODY INTO
TURNAROUND PASSES:*** *Body
position is most important on a
turnaround type of pass pattern.
The receiver first "addresses the
quarterback" by coming back
toward the ball (7-22), allowing his
body to shield the defender from
the ball (7-23) while he makes the
catch and secures the ball (7-24).*

FIGURE 7-25

FIGURE 7-26

MAKING THE DEEP CATCH: *To position his body to catch a pass on a deep pattern, the receiver holds off the defender with his body (7-25), forcing him to have to go through him if he wants to make a play. He catches the ball with his arms extended (7-26 & 7-27) and secures the ball while running (7-28).*

FIGURE 7-27

FIGURE 7-28

Receivers, particularly after they have just caught a pass, are seen as potential victims to defensive players, who always are trying to knock that ball lose to cause an incompletion or create a turnover. So the receiver must take instant care to put the ball away safely after he has caught it—to take it from his hands and tuck it in a football carrying position. The back point of the ball should fit snugly up under the armpit, and the front tip of the ball should be secured by the receiver's hand.

A serious word of caution: do not carry the ball under the point because a glancing blow can knock it loose, and every defender is looking for get-even time. If the defender can force the ball to pop free, then he may go from goat to hero in an instant. The greatest run in the world is useless if it ends with the defense falling on a fumble because the receiver failed to put the ball away and protect it.

Tucking the ball away must happen in an instant, and it must occur even before the receiver begins to run. Again, this falls under the category of *mental concentration*. At every level of competition receivers make the mistake of thinking about the big play when their first thought must be of catching the ball and the second about putting it away. Then, and only then, can they think about the big play.

A receiver also must pay attention to protecting the ball while running. If he has it in his left arm, the left hand is over the point of the ball. When he is about to be tackled, he must cover it with both hands, thus reducing any chance of the ball being stripped from his possession.

This is the time to begin to develop those essential mental work habits, and it can be more easily accomplished by following this sequence:

1. Get off the line of scrimmage,
2. Beat the defender,
3. Get to the break point at the proper time,
4. Adjust to the defense,
5. Catch the football,
6. Tuck it away securely, and
7. Run with the ball.

Running After the Catch

Not every player who carries a football is a great runner, and the ones who are usually wind up as running backs. But receivers must have some kind of feeling for running after the catch, and that "feel" really is following a logical set of principles that add up to one thing—going *down* the field.

"Down the field" is important, as was demonstrated by all the great runners like O. J. Simpson, Jim Brown and Walter Payton. When they got into traffic, they never headed for the sidelines (unless they knew they could outrun the defender) but instead headed toward the goal line to make as much yardage as they could. Receivers must do the same thing, even though instead of wide open spaces or clear paths to the end zone, there will be a hungry, converging band of defenders anxious to level the receiver before he can get started.

Here, the game becomes one of angles, with receivers working to position themselves to get nothing but glancing blows coming from an angle. First of all, this means not running "dumb-tough" or trying to run over a defender. It also means not trying too many jitterbug-ging moves, because this means the receiver is standing still, moving only his feet, and giving time for the defensive pursuit to catch him.

Instead, the receiver should try to head straight down the field toward the end zone, trying to split the defenders by running between two converging tacklers. If he bears to the right, that defender will nail him; the same thing will happen if he runs to the left. But by splitting them, he will get hit at an angle and be able, from the force of his forward momentum, to fall forward for a few more yards. It is sometimes surprising how much those "few more yards" add up over the course of a season and how often they mean the difference in a tight game.

Now if the receiver is confronted after the catch by only one defender, then he must try to beat him quickly before the defensive pursuit arrives. One quick move is about all the receiver will get, so it must be decisive, and after that, he runs for as much yardage as he can get.

A receiver should be cautioned not to lose ground to gain ground. When running with the ball, he should avoid dipping back toward the line of scrimmage to make someone miss a tackle. More often than not, the pursuit will get into the play and the result will be a loss of the yardage the receiver had already gained. Get positive yardage with every move!

Should the receiver have room to run, he can go as fast as he can but he should have his *body under control* when he makes cuts, just as when he runs a pass pattern. He cannot break off and change direction in a pattern going at full speed, so, too, must he slow down when he makes his cuts to avoid tacklers. Good runners—not necessarily the fastest ones—have a series of "gears," in which they slow down or speed up, depending upon the traffic around them, to help them avoid tacklers. These "gear changes" are never done at full speed but always with measured control. A pass receiver can do the same thing by staying under control, seeing the field and always working his way downfield.

FIGURE 7-29

RUNNING WITH THE BALL: *When a receiver runs with the ball, he must have it securely held in his body with both hands (7-29), and then as the defenders are about to tackle him (7-30), he forces them to hit him from*

FIGURE 7-32

FIGURE 7-30   **FIGURE 7-31**

the side so that he can split them and make additional yards while
being tackled (7-31–7-33).

FIGURE 7-33

Of course, a receiver should take advantage of any opportunities to make defenders miss him in the open field. Again, this is similar to running a pass pattern because the receiver wants the defender to believe he is going one way, when in fact, he plans on going in another direction. If the receiver simply runs straight and turns without giving that defender a move, he won't get very far. But if he gives him a false step to get him going one way, then shifts in another direction, he might get some running room. All of this depends on what the receiver sees, and the better field, or peripheral, vision he has, the more of the field he will see, and the more potential tacklers will pop into his vision—then he can fall back on his ability to use his quickness and change of direction. If he can change direction faster than the defender, he'll make him miss.

A Pass Receiver's Top 20 Principles

1. Get better every day. Practice to overcome your weaknesses, not just to increase your strengths.

2. Always run your patterns as if you are the No. 1 receiver. In practice, run patterns at full speed because you cannot get the correct timing at half speed.

3. Know your adjustments and have a mental picture of what you must do and what your options are. Be prepared to react instinctively, because the time it takes you to think about what you do can cost you a catch.

4. Know your adjustments and always expect the worst so you won't be surprised. Prepare for any circumstance.

5. In practice, after you catch the ball, tuck it away quickly and securely, and sprint upfield for at least ten yards. Add a fake, a spin, or some other move to simulate what you would do in a game. Get positive yardage. Split the defenders to get those extra couple of yards.

6. Concentrate at all times on what you are going to do and why and how you are going to do it. Keep in mind the overall pattern and what your part of it is. Know what your pattern adjustments are.

7. Vary your techniques of releasing off the line of scrimmage so defenders don't get a "book" on you and devise a plan to keep you from getting into a pattern. You won't get the ball if you're still on the line of scrimmage.

8. Once off the line of scrimmage, your first concern is to determine if the coverage is man or zone.

9. See the nearest three defenders to help read coverages. Get your pre-snap read first, then read coverage on the move. You must know your coverage keys.

10. Attack the defender by running patterns "into his technique," to scare him with the feeling you are attacking his area of responsibility.

11. Master and use the tools to get open, and be *where* you are supposed to be, *when* you are supposed to be there.

12. Keep your eyes on the ball. Your first responsibility is to catch the ball. After you catch it think about two things—more yardage and scoring.

13. Always be alert for the ball, even though you are not the primary receiver. You never know when the quarterback will throw to you, so assume you're "the guy."

14. Every receiver must be considered eligible, and no one in a pattern ever should consider himself a "decoy."

15. Form the habit of going all-out after the ball every time, regardless of how or where it is thrown.

16. The sidelines and end lines are your enemies. Always know your relative position to them. Respect them, but do not let them bother you when catching the ball. The catch comes first!

17. Put a "deep feeling" into your pass route and make the defender think you are going deep on your breaking patterns to create a cushion. Then "burst" to get into position to catch the ball.

18. A receiver must develop the ability to "address the ball" or work back toward the quarterback to catch the ball.

19. Receivers are football players, not just pass catchers, so you must block. When you see the ball thrown to another receiver, you instantly become a blocker. Pick somebody out, starting with the man who is covering you. Take pride in helping each other.

20. There is no "free ball" on offense. It belongs to your team so go get it! Never allow an interception. If you must play defense, do it.

SECTION THREE
Putting the Quarterback and the Receiver Together

The basic philosophy of any passing offense should be, we will take any completion we can get.

In Cincinnati, the Bengals have one of the NFL's most exciting pass offenses, and we regularly feature long-distance strikes to such gifted and speedy receivers as Eddie Brown and Tim McGee. Yet, we are never too proud to consider that a pass can be as much of a scoring weapon from inside the ten-yard line as a run by Ickey Woods or James Brooks. To give you a good example, in our 1988 Super Bowl season, we had a half dozen touchdown pass plays of over fifty yards, but we also had eight from inside the ten-yard line, including four that traveled five yards or less. The message here is, a forward pass is a good weapon from any place on the football field.

Throwing the ball is one thing, but where the ball goes and when is the key to maintaining a consistent pass offense. This begins with the talent at hand. If the quarterback can throw long and short with good accuracy, then the coach has many passing weapons at his disposal. If the quarterback does not have great arm strength, then it would be foolish to rely on a long-passing game. Instead, the coach must construct an offense that best suits the physical abilities of his passer. The Bengals had a quarterback named Virgil Carter back in 1970, the third year of the team's existence, who was only an average passer and who never really terrorized the deep areas of any NFL secondaries. So our defensive staff constructed a short-passing offense that was good enough to help Virgil win the last seven games of the year and allow us to become the earliest playoff participant by any NFL expansion team.

Coaches who draw up their game plans should follow the same rule when looking for weaknesses to exploit. If the opponent has a slow cornerback, then the fastest receiver should be working against him. If an opponent has a great run defense, then the coach should find a way to use his passing game to open up areas for the running backs. Again it goes back to the rule we started at the beginning of this section: we will take any completion we can get. Regardless of the level of competition, that is a good rule to follow.

VIII. Out-Thinking the Defense

Ken Anderson was never worried about making the big plays—and he got plenty of them during his NFL career. He always felt that a four-yard gain from a pass completion on first down was a good play because at second-and-six, he still had plenty of options to either run or pass the ball. So, rather than searching for a receiver to come open for more yardage on the first down, he often hit that first open receiver to get something started. He wanted the sure yardage.

We will take any completion we can get.

Many young quarterbacks who want to make only big, exciting plays may selfishly ignore receivers who run shorter patterns, even if they are the top choices on their progression list, and spend all of their time in the pocket looking for the deep receiver. And when that deep guy doesn't come open, then what do they do? If the quarterback goes back to look for the first couple of receivers who may have been open when the play began, he'll probably find that they're covered. By then, the defensive pass rush also has closed in so there is only time to throw the ball away, try to scramble for yardage, or most likely, get sacked—three pretty horrible possibilities.

The message here is that both coach and quarterback should not be greedy.

Of course, at the same time, they should not be lashed down to a style that never puts the ball deep downfield on first down. Ken utilized the best combination. He had patience that allowed his passing game to get a maximum number of completions whenever possible, and he was always ready to go deep when the defense presented the opportunity. Often, the deep pass on first down will succeed because of earlier shorter completions on first down that lulled the defense into squatting on receivers, leaving the deeper secondary open. An occasional deep throw also makes the defense nervous, particularly if it succeeds. The defense will back up, allowing other areas to open up. If the quarterback begins clicking in shorter areas, pretty soon the defense will begin to creep up, again leaving the opportunity open for a deep strike.

Play selection in the passing game should center around choosing the correct pattern for the correct situation. At the start of every series, the advantage usually rests with the offense because the defense doesn't really know what is coming. Generally, on first down, the defense looks to play the run so their linebackers are closer to the line and their defensive backs are looking to the corners where they might be called upon to force running plays to the inside. This is a good time to run pass patterns behind the linebackers and into the middle of the field, or it may be good to use some play action and send a receiver or two deep, particularly if the running game is perking on first down and occupying the defensive backs in run support.

On other downs, the defense will look at how many yards are needed for a first down and set their defenses accordingly. If it is second-and-eight, the defense will be thinking about stopping longer passes. If the quarterback sends a receiver into an area of less than eight yards and he catches a pass, it is because the defense has chosen to cover the deeper areas, believing that is where the ball will go. Now the quarterback has made a play, no matter how small, and his third down problem has lessened.

Of course, if it is third-and-fourteen, the quarterback must have a pattern that will go farther than fourteen yards. However, if the quarterback sees his receiver covered, he still cannot force the ball to him because he risks two mishaps—an interception or an incompletion. Instead, he should look elsewhere, and if an outlet receiver is free eight yards down field, he should be thrown the ball. Who knows? The receiver might break free and make up the distance, and at the least, the yardage gained can be tacked onto the team's punting total, getting the ball that much deeper into enemy territory. Football still is a team game, and no single unit—and certainly no single player, particularly the quarterback—must feel a total responsibility.

Read the Defense

While young quarterbacks and receivers are just becoming familiar with the intracacies of a pass offense as they master the requirements of each pattern, neither one can ever ignore the burdens placed upon them by the opposing defense. At this level of competition, those burdens will most likely take two basic forms, *man-to-man* and *zone* coverage.

Beating Man-to-Man Defense

This is the most effective pass defense, if a team has the athletes who can do the job, because the receiver will never really be open. Two cornerbacks are assigned to cover the two wide receivers, the strong safety and the linebacker facing him will cover the tight end, and the two other linebackers will cover the other two running backs. The free safety will patrol the middle of the field and he will help one of the other defenders, most often either of the cornerbacks. Knowing this is one thing—recognizing it is something else. Here are some tips:

1. Check the position of the cornerbacks while the signals are being called. If they are playing a bit tighter to the line of scrimmage, they most likely are looking to cover a specific receiver and do not want him to get away too quickly.

2. If the linebackers move sideways to cover a running back or check his movements before going to help in other coverage, they are in man coverage. In zone defense, they normally move away from the line of scrimmage at an angle to get into area coverage.

What will work against this coverage?

Let's start with the placement of *running backs*. They usually are faster and more elusive than linebackers, so try and isolate a back on a linebacker. *Wide receivers* can utilize the "move" patterns such as the crossing patterns and the down-and-ins and down-and-outs. All of these are designed to get a step on the defender and into open territory where the receiver can catch the ball on the run. The crossing pattern is very effective because the receiver can run under the ball.

One of the keys to success against man-to-man coverage is getting *single coverage* by the defense on a receiver. The *free safety's* role is key here because he is the player designated to help out on coverage, often against the most dangerous receiver, and the quarterback must be aware of his presence at all times. The free safety looks for the cornerbacks to funnel receivers into his middle area. A receiver running a crossing pattern, ahead a step or two on the cornerback, may suddenly find himself picked up by the free safety. The quarterback must be sure before he throws the ball that his receiver indeed is free of that inside coverage. As long as the quarterback has time to sit back in the pocket and scan the field for the double coverage, he will have the option of getting a receiver in single coverage.

But it's not always this easy. If a defense has talented people, it may utilize *combinations* with its man-to-man coverage. This could involve using two safeties on the tight end if he is swift and a good receiver or putting a linebacker with the strong safety or having two linebackers cover a running back if the other running back stays in to block. But receivers have the responsibility of trying to free themselves of all coverage by the manner in which they run their patterns.

The quarterback also must beware of one other potential enemy—

himself, particularly his *eyes*, and this is true whether the coverage is man-to-man or zone. This is a problem at every level of the game, and in the NFL there are talented quarterbacks who constantly fight the habit of tracking their prime receiver across the field before they throw him the ball. That is one of a defense's great keys because the quarterback really is tipping off who his receiver will be and where the ball will be thrown. In man-to-man defense, the free safety will look in at the quarterback first to pick up that key and if the eyes are locked onto a particular receiver, he will head for him.

Of course, a quarterback cannot throw the ball to a spot that he is not watching, nor can he watch that receiver from the moment he leaves the line of scrimmage. So he should scan the entire field before focusing on his primary receiver. That scanning will help him if he must go to other receivers if his first choice target is covered, and it will not tip off his intentions. But the "eye habit" is very easy for a young quarterback to fall into, and it is something he must work to overcome in every practice session.

Beating a Zone Defense

The zone defense covers different areas, or zones, of the field and is designed to keep everything in front of it, while giving up ground gradually, if at all, hoping that eventually the offense will break down and turn the ball over.

Defensive players are assigned coverage responsibility within those zones. On the snap of the ball, the linebackers and defensive backs move immediately into those areas. The areas between the zones are known as "seams" and they are the spots where receivers and quarterbacks should look for openings.

How can a quarterback recognize whether the defense will be zone or man-to-man? The key is watching the safeties. If they move to an area—and if the linebackers drop back to their areas—then the zone defense is being formed. If the free safety stays in the middle of the field, and if the linebackers move to cover a tight end or running back, then they are going in man-to-man defense. But once the quarterback sees the zone defense form, he can expect one of the two following strategies:

1. *Strong-Side Zone.* Three defensive backs and two linebackers move toward the side of the offensive formation where the tight end and flanker are located. A team that features its tight end or moves its receivers to that side of the field can expect a lot of strong side zone coverage.

2. *Weak-Side Zone.* The defensive backs and linebackers will move toward the weak side of the offensive formation, or away from the tight end and flanker. The clue will be when the strong safety

moves toward the center of the field, and the weak safety rolls toward the weak side of the formation. Defenses facing a fine receiver who works from the weak side of the formation favor this alignment.

How does a quarterback cope with this kind of defense? First of all, he must have patience. One of the great psychological weapons in a zone defense is that the quarterback will get so frustrated by not having his receivers running free through a secondary that he will try to force a ball down the field and into an area of coverage where the defender has room to snare it. He must be patient and satisfied with anything the zone defense is giving him, yet not be too timid that he will be content with a dink-and-dunk offense that doesn't produce first downs.

He must also work in areas *underneath and between the zones*, where there may not be spectacular plays but enough yardage to keep the offense moving and accumulating first downs. Now, if the quarterback can get good pass protection, his receivers can expand those zones and open up areas in the "seams" where the ball can go for larger gains.

If the quarterback sees the defense going into either weak-side or strong-side zone coverage, then he should look to the opposite side because there will be more room and fewer defenders. He should also look down the middle of the field, where tight ends can often run free through the seams while the zones swallow up the wide receivers.

Finally, there is the running game. While we talk throughout this book about the merits of the passing game, by no means do we ever want to ignore the importance of the run. If a team can establish a strong running game, then it will have the defense off balance and vulnerable to the pass. When a zone defense has trouble coping with the run, the linebackers become vulnerable since they are more run conscious and are ripe for some play-action moves that will freeze them from retreating into their coverage areas. Those areas come open for receivers working in front of the secondary.

The Receiver's Responsibility

While the quarterback is primarily responsible for recognizing the zone defense, the responsibility for getting open falls primarily on the receivers. He must find the seams or open areas on the field and get into them. At the same time, the quarterback must also recognize those open areas and "think along" with the receiver.

There are ways to do that. If the quarterback spots a strong-side zone defense, he can throw weak-side patterns with a halfback stopping in the area between two linebackers, the split end curling in behind the linebacker and the tight end going into the middle between defenders. The quarterback also can have a running back come into an area in front of a linebacker to influence his movements—"clearing out" is the popular term—and then have the split end come into that area. A good comeback pattern is effective here.

Nor should the quarterback and receiver totally ignore the long pass, even if the basic philosophy of working against a zone is to take what it gives. If a team plays strong-side zone coverage, a speedy split end has a chance to run past the weak-side cornerback. Or if the quarterback plans to throw over the middle, he should have one receiver going down the middle to occupy the weak safety so another receiver can work in front of him. The ideal is to have receivers in short, medium and long ranges to stretch those zones; then the quarterback throws to the receiver who is open.

There are also times when a quarterback finds a defense "playing plays," or anticipating that one receiver will get the ball. This happens if teams play each other a couple of times a year and become familiar with tendencies. They believe they know what a team will do in certain situations and which receiver will get the ball, so they ignore the other receivers. Here is where a receiver can help the cause by telling his quarterback or coach that he is being ignored. That is a good time to fake one of those plays the defense anticipates and then bring another receiver into the area that has been vacated. That is when both receiver and quarterback may find that "big play" for which they have been searching.

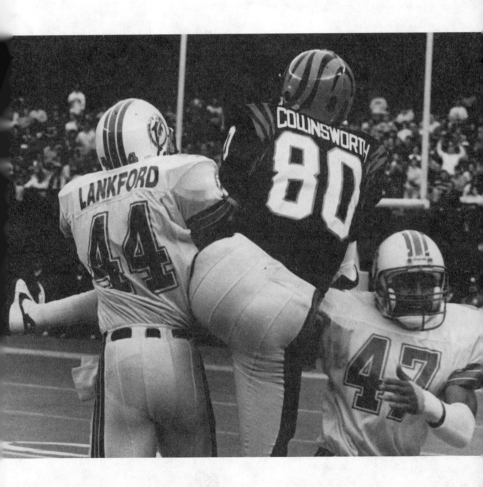

IX. Throwing the Ball and Catching It

The quarterback and his receivers must work as a well-coordinated team, because everything the quarterback does is complemented by what the receiver does.

But even before the ball is thrown, indeed, even before the players step onto the field, every player must have had enough preparation to ensure that the hoped-for teamwork will become reality. The pressure in a game simply does not allow players to succeed without sufficient preparation, particularly in critical situations where split-second decisions are required. Then each player must react to each situation and do what is necessary to succeed...and do it correctly. In other words, you can't make it up as you go along!

This comes under the category of "being a smart player." The quarterback must know which receivers he can rely on in tight situations, and the receivers must know how to make error-free plays. All this learning takes place during practice sessions so that the players have a reservoir of knowledge ready to apply in an instant.

Players have the responsibility of pouring as much energy as is feasible into their pre-game preparation, but young high school and youth league players must remember that schoolwork takes precedence over football. Both are possible, however, if young players get sufficient rest and relaxation to lead a balanced life where football is only one part.

Throwing the Ball

Before discussing the various pass patterns and how to use them, the quarterback and receiver must understand what happens when the ball is thrown, and the best way to make each throw successful. Part of that success concerns *the ball's path*—how it travels after it leaves the quarterback's hands.

Ken Anderson's preference always was to throw the ball low and allow his receivers to go to the ground to make the catch, unless a receiver was wide open. Then he got the ball where it was easily caught so he could keep running.

In either case, the key was finding a safe spot to place the ball.

Balls were thrown low so the receivers would not have to take severe punishment from behind, where they are open targets to eager defensive backs looking to knock the ball loose after a catch or before the ball is secured. Quarterbacks should avoid throwing passes where the receiver must stretch to make the catch, because that leaves the receiver defenseless in protecting his body and thus susceptible to injury. The ball also should be aimed low and away from the defender if there is any doubt about whether it will be completed, making certain that if the receiver can't make the catch, then neither can the defender.

The receiver also must give the quarterback a good target with his hands whenever possible, remembering to use either the "thumbs together" or "little fingers together" style, which we discussed earlier in the book.

The receiver also must be able to adjust to balls that are not perfectly thrown, as we also noted earlier in the book. Instead of just reaching back to snare balls thrown behind him, he must actually turn his body by placing his front foot in the direction in which he is going, and moving the back foot to open his hips and moving them out of the way. This will provide his hands with some room to "give" with the catch. Remember, the ball comes in with a certain velocity and if it hits a flat surface that doesn't move—in this case, the hips—it will just bounce away.

It is the same for low throws, where bending the legs gets the knees out of the way. If the receiver keeps his legs together or bends from the waist, he cannot achieve that necessary cradling action, but if he bends down in a squatting position, the legs have to come open, leaving him room to form a cradle for the ball with his arms and hands.

When the quarterback faces a first-and-20 or first-and-25 situation, he shouldn't panic and try to get it all with one big throw. The defense will set up in order to take away such a play, but in so doing, it also may leave open shorter areas. Enough short completions can soon add up to what is needed for a first down. The key is to get something right away to lessen the yardage figure and keep the pressure on the defense. Of course, if the quarterback is facing a second or third down, with 20 or 25 yards to gain, then, depending upon field position, he must put the ball farther down the field. He also must have receivers in the game who can make longer plays.

If it gets to be third and less than ten yards, he probably will face more man-to-man coverge, so the quarterback can go to an individual pass route, such as the crossing pattern.

The Pass Patterns

Slant

This pattern is run with a three-step drop by the quarterback and is very effective against man-to-man coverage, especially if there is a swift receiver against a slower defender. This is what we call a "step" pattern. The receiver runs five steps upfield, plants his outside foot, and angles or "slants" to the middle of the field. All the receiver needs is one step on the defender and the ball delivered where he can catch it while running at full speed. The ball should be thrown out front but also a bit low so the receiver won't have to take a solid head-on hit by the defender. Keep this pass in mind on first down near the goal line where the quarterback can use play action to freeze the linebacker and throw the slant behind him.

Against a zone defense, the linebacker probably will drop straight back and the strong safety will slide to the outside. The area between them will be "soft" and a good area for the receiver to get open.

Post

This works off the slant because the two are almost the same except this pattern is run deeper. The pattern is thrown off a five-step drop, and its route is angled toward the goal post, hence its name. The key to completion is putting the ball out in front of the receiver and allowing him to run under it. If he must run all out to get it, then he hopefully can get distance from the defender. If the ball is thrown too short, the receiver will have to stop or slow down, and the defender can get into the play. Also the ball should be thrown on an angle to the goal posts so it will be carried away from the defender.

Ken Anderson was reluctant to throw the post pattern if there was a free safety in coverage, while Dan Fouts, when he played for the San Diego Chargers, often did it by taking a short drop and letting the ball fly to one of his fastest receivers, figuring the receiver might, through the element of surprise, zoom past the free safety and run under the ball.

Against a zone defense, the play should work off the cornerback and free safety because the soft part of the zone will be between them. Some teams make this pattern an "automatic" against certain types of blitzes because the secondary may be forced into single coverage, getting the free safety away from the middle of the field, and the quarterback can throw it on a quick, three-step drop.

Out

There are two kinds of out patterns, the square-out and the quick-out. The *square-out* is a 10 to 12-yard pattern, thrown off a five-step drop. It also is a timing pattern, and the ball must be released before the receiver breaks so the defensive back does not have time to react. The receiver's "burst" is important here because he must drive the defender back before breaking to the outside. The receiver must angle back toward the sideline to catch the ball before the defensive back can recover and make a play.

The *quick-out* is a timing pattern thrown off a three-step drop. The receiver shortens his route to only five yards before making his cut and working back toward the sideline. Again, the "burst" is important to drive the defender backward, and the quarterback again should deliver the ball low and out in front so the receiver must come back to catch it. Against a zone defense, the strong safety will "buzz" or sprint to the outside, and the ball must get to the receiver before he can recover and get into the play.

Cross

In the pros this is a 15-to 20-yard pattern that can be shortened up at the younger levels of competition to accommodate a young quarterback's arm strength and accuracy. Of course, if he can do it in 15 or 20 yards, that's fine. The pass works well off an "out" pattern because the defense is conscious of it, but now the receiver runs straight down the sideline and then breaks across the middle as the quarterback throws from a maximum drop (five steps at this level).

How the ball is thrown depends upon the coverage. Against man-to-man, the ball should lead the receiver away from the defender and be thrown low so the receiver will not get struck full force by the free safety coming over to make a play; in zone coverage, the strong safety may move to take away the out so the receiver comes straight up and turns inside. When the strong safety overplays the outside to take away that "out" pattern, he helps this pattern succeed. The linebacker will drop to the area where the strong safety was, so the soft part of the zone occurs in the area between the linebacker and the cornerback. If the wide receiver gets there too early, he must slow down since the quarterback will not throw the ball until he sees the strong safety out of the area. If the receiver is going to be in a tight spot between defenders, the pass must fall under a category known as "touch." This means that it must be feathered over the linebacker's head, therefore coming in at a slower velocity but with enough "touch" that it clears the linebacker's upstretched arms and gets to the receiver lower and in front of the cornerback and other safety. Of course, if there is no free safety then the quarterback can get the ball up and allow his receiver to make the catch on the run, and he'll get a big play.

Hook

The receiver runs a route about 16 yards downfield and hooks between the linebackers in the zone. The quarterback must throw the ball low, so the receiver makes his body bigger to protect it from the defensive back who really must come through him to make a play. There also is an *"adjust hook"* pass that can be used against a zone defense in which the wide receiver works to either side of the strong safety and hooks in front of the cornerback. In so doing, he must convince the corner that he will be going deep and make a good burst before making his cut. Against a man-to-man defense, the receiver can beat the defender with the pattern, making an adjustment on where and how he hooks. This is a great call against a defense that doesn't have any underneath help.

Streak

Also known as a "Go," this works well off a hook pattern that has burned the defense a couple of times because the cornerback drove up to make the play. In running the streak, the receiver should simulate the start of the hook or out pattern to influence that antsy corner. But instead of hooking or running an out, he executes a good burst and goes right past that corner. Often, a quarterback will simply throw the ball as far as he can, hoping the receiver can run under the ball behind the defense. The quarterback will wait, if he has good protection, and let the receiver get a good start before lofting the ball and allowing him to run under it.

However, how far the ball is thrown is not as important as the technique in throwing it and when it should be thrown. Ken Anderson always threw the ball high and to the outside, "with some air under it," so it came in over the receiver's outside shoulder as he faded away toward the sideline. This gave him an opportunity to make his body bigger and to protect the ball. Against a zone defense, the quarterback doesn't have to worry about underneath coverage, only the action of the cornerback and his depth in the secondary. If the cornerbacks are deep, this pattern shouldn't be thrown because the receiver probably won't be able to outrun them. This pattern should be used off successful hook and out patterns, if the cornerbacks crowd the line of scrimmage, or if a speedy receiver can overwhelm a slower corner.

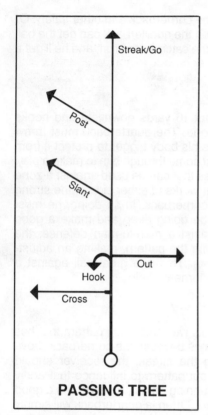

Streak/Go

Post

Slant

Out

Hook

Cross

PASSING TREE

THE PASSING TREE: The Passing Tree, with the various routes appearing as branches. Obviously, these routes can be run in opposite directions simply by turning the tree around.

Swing Pass

This is thrown to a running back running toward the sideline after he makes a bit of a swing, or "belly" route and then straightens his direction so he will be able to catch the ball at full stride going downfield. The ball must be delivered so the back won't have to break stride to catch it, and it should be thrown at medium speed because he will be relatively close to the passer. This is a good pass at the bottom of a progression list when all other receivers are covered. But it requires work to make the timing error-free so tipped balls won't fall into the hands of pursuing linebackers.

Screen Pass

The quarterback must be a good actor for this pattern, and he must "sell" the pass by looking downfield as if searching for a receiver. Then he lofts the ball to one of his backs, who then runs behind a protective screen of blocking linemen.

This back should set up before the pass as if to block. Then he slides behind the linemen after they have released their blocks. The quarterback, meanwhile, should slowly drift back and bring the pass rushers away from the screen of blockers. If he doesn't sell the deception with his eyes and backward movements the defensive guys will smell the deception and break back to cover the play. The quarterback must also keep sight of his receiver and be certain that he is clear to catch the ball. Sometimes a back can get knocked down in all the traffic or be covered by a defender who has smelled out the ruse. In that case, the quarterback must throw the ball away, if he has time, or just take the sack. He also must have courage to throw this pattern, because once his linemen release their blocks, those defensive linemen will come all out. He must time his throw so that it goes over their hands before they get too close, and he cannot flinch because he may get knocked down.

Some Strategical Don'ts

In preparing for a game, there sometimes is a temptation to succumb to an old, but oh so erroneous notion of using a top receiver as a "decoy." If a team does that, it takes a prime weapon out of the game and does the defense a huge favor. Sure, that receiver will get special coverage, but it is up to the offense to find a way to get him the ball. Throw it to him and make the defense play him, because great players are rarely shut down. If that player just runs up and down the field without seeing the ball, it won't take the defense long to figure out he has not been included in the game plan, and they can shift coverage against the other players.

There also is an erroneous notion that once a play begins to work successfully, it shouldn't be used too often lest the defense catch on and make some changes. The defense already knows it is being burned, and it can only hope that the offense will come off that play and do something else it can better handle. If a play is working, stay with it and force the defense to stop it. If it can't, then the offense is in good shape. If it does, perhaps by that time it will be too late.

Receivers Must Block, Too

Receivers are in a game to catch the football but they also are required to block on running plays or when other receivers catch the ball. There are two kinds of effective blocks by receivers: the stalk block and the cut block.

FIGURE 9-1

STALK BLOCKING: *The blocker closes on a defender as the ball carrier follows his path (9-1). He fronts him in a fundamental football position with legs bent and makes contact only when the defender starts to make a play on the ball carrier (9-2), maintaining contact and moving the defender in the direction he tries to go as the runner cuts off the block (9-3).*

Stalk Block

This block uses the receiver's prime weapons—speed and quickness—so he should be a good enough athlete to stay in front of someone and prevent him from making a tackle.

He must come off the line of scrimmage and use his body language just as if he were running a pattern, getting the defender to backpedal. The farther he can take him from where the ball will be run, the better he is doing his job. He must get in front of that defender—stalk him. When he finally gets close to him, he must get into a fundamental football position—just like a basketball player on defense where he mirrors every move of the ball carrier. When that defender makes a move to tackle the runner, then the receiver shoulder blocks him, placing his head across the path the defender is trying to go.

However, the important part of this technique is timing. The

FIGURE 9-2

FIGURE 9-3

receiver cannot hit him right away because the defensive back could throw him off and still have time to make the tackle. He never should lunge either but instead keep his body weight over his feet. If the receiver overextends, the defender will grab him and throw him aside.

Cut Block

This is a one-shot deal, and it doesn't work too well against an athlete with great reactions. If he is cut too early, he can get up and make the tackle. But the block is a good change-of-pace weapon if the receiver has used a stalk block several times in a row.

The receiver must come hard off the line of scrimmage as if running a pattern, selling the idea with his body language, and then make the defender believe he will use a stalk block. When he is within two yards of the defender, he must hit him by lunging with a straight back and cutting up and through the defender's thigh pad. That thigh pad is the target of the block. If he cuts him too low to the ground, the defender can jump over him; if he gets him around the midsection, he can bounce off. If he cuts him on the way down, the defender can push him into the ground, or the receiver could duck his head with that move and miss the block altogether.

The receiver not only blocks on runs but he also must be prepared to do so on passes. When he doesn't get the ball, he becomes a blocker the moment he sees the ball in the air. He must turn and block the closest defender. It is all in a day's work.

X. Drills to Excel

Good passers and receivers are like diamonds just brought from a mine. They need to be polished to become valuable.

Polishing means working to improve techniques to a point where they become almost automatic during a game. This polishing process is not limited only to those players who are deftly skilled; both ordinary and struggling players may also polish to become better players.

Drills can be practiced at any time, so a player can continue a path of development and not have to start over every fall. If any young quarterback or receiver is serious about advancing his skills, then he should be charting a course that allows him to work at the game in and out of season.

Drills for the Quarterback

Since throwing the football is where it all begins, a quarterback must be precise every time he does so, whether in a game, in warm up, in practice or just playing catch. There should be a purpose with every toss, and the main one is *improving accuracy*. Simply warming up may not seem important to many, but good habits will unquestionably carry over to the field. There are some who claim that a quarterback will be happy in a game just to throw near a receiver and therefore only needs to aim for the body in warm up. Nonsense! Accuracy with every throw, under any conditions, must be the primary objective.

Be specific when throwing the ball. If the person receiving the throw is wearing a helmet, pick out the face mask and aim for it with every throw. The more refined the throw, the more accurate it will become.

Here are some drills that will help a young quarterback begin to develop his accuracy:

Throw on the Run

In the levels below pro football, the ability to throw on the run is particularly important, because sprint-out quarterbacks are used quite a bit. We have already touched on the technique of throwing on the run—not leading the receiver but throwing the ball directly at

FIGURE 10-1

THROW ON THE RUN: *Ken, as the quarterback, and Matt, the receiver, set themselves 10 yards apart and begin to run in the same direction (10-1). Ken opens his shoulders and throws the ball directly at Matt (10-2) as they run along throwing the ball back and forth. (10-3–10-5).*

him—and a fine drill to help perfect that technique is to find a partner, set yourselves ten yards apart, and run up and down throwing the ball to each other.

In so doing, concentrate on getting the shoulders open to the target and throw directly at it. Not only does this polish a throwing skill, but it also helps with conditioning, particularly after practice when a coach may wish his quarterbacks to do something more useful than running sprints.

Touch Drill

This can pay dividends whenever a quarterback must scramble and still try to complete a pass that needs a delicate touch, over the linebackers and in front of the defensive backs. Start on a line ten yards in front of the goal posts and station someone behind them to catch the ball. Run from the right and then from the left and loft the ball over the crossbar. This creates a situation where the ball must go up and drop over something.

FIGURE 10-2

FIGURE 10-3

FIGURE 10-4

FIGURE 10-5

This is not something that young quarterbacks can expect to perfect as soon as they start out, but once they get proficient at passing from the pocket and begin to utilize roll-out passes, this will help get the ball into tight places.

Throw Off the Knee

This is a two-purpose drill. Place the right knee on the ground and play catch with someone. Throw to the right, center and left, opening the shoulders to face the target with each throw. This improves the throwing technique and is a good way to warm up before practice. It can also be done standing up, with the feet together, which gets the thrower used to rotating his body to face his target.

Front-Foot Drill

This will help you throw with a straight downward motion. Rise up on your toes and go through the throwing motion, effecting a weight transfer from the right to the left foot (vice versa for left-handed throwers). Bring the ball forward with a straight overhand motion. This will develop good habits, particularly when throwing the ball over the middle. A passer who, instead, throws flat-footed will often see his ball take off instead of going down toward the receiver.

This drill has one other advantage. By rising up on his toes, the quarterback gets about two inches taller. Otherwise, if the passer extends too far out with his feet planted solidly on the ground, he actually loses inches from the natural top of his throwing arc, and that's when balls get batted down, or worse yet, intercepted.

Drills for Receivers

Since a receiver must be most concerned with how he catches the ball—and whether he does it consistently under all types of conditions—then he should school himself to become as competent as possible. That brings us to two premises:

1. A receiver can never catch too many balls.
2. In every practice or drill, everything should be done as it would be in a game. That means that receivers, too, should make every effort to polish their skills each time they catch a ball—whether it is in practice or just playing catch. If a receiver is playing catch or warming up a quarterback, he should be sure to catch every ball in his hands, secure it and tuck it away, just as he would do in a game. This will get him into a habit and will cut down on potential fumbles or dropped passes.

FIGURE 10-6

TOUCH DRILL: *Ken stands ten yards in front of the goal post (10-6) and throws a ball to a player stationed behind it (10-7), taking care to throw*

FIGURE 10-8

FIGURE 10-7

it as close to the crossbar (10-8 & 10-9) to simulate getting it into a tight spot between a linebacker and defensive back.

FIGURE 10-9

FIGURE 10-10   **FIGURE 10-11**

FRONT FOOT DRILL: *Ken stands on his toes (10-10) with the ball cocked behind his head and brings the ball forward in a straight overhand motion (10-11).*

In other words, don't look upon a game of catch as nothing more than an idle pastime. Put it to work, and make even these modest efforts pay off.

During our daily practice session with the Bengals, we put our receivers through a series of basic drills aimed at keeping them sharp and fundamentally sound. These are work sessions, and if a player does not perform correctly, then the drill is stopped and he is corrected. Even professional players are never too good not to learn more and polish their talents.

Here are four good drills for receivers at any level of competition.

Sideline Drill

This will help you use the sideline under control. It is a very good drill for mastering the out patterns that carry a receiver close to the sideline before he catches the ball, when he must worry about keeping his feet in bounds while at the same time focusing on securing the ball.

Run the out, starting quickly and getting into the out move. The

FIGURE 10-12

FIGURE 10-13

FIGURE 10-14

SIDELINE DRILL: *J.J. breaks toward the sideline (10-12) and then concentrates on catching the ball (10-13) while also keeping his feet in bounds (10-14).*

FIGURE 10-15   **FIGURE 10-16**

BAD BALL DRILL (High Throw): J.J. *runs down the field, then breaks to the inside (10-15–10-17) as the ball is thrown above his head, forcing him to reach for it (10-18). He concentrates on the ball as he brings it into his middle (10-19) and puts it away while beginning to run (10-20).*

passer should throw the ball, aiming for out of bounds. There are three things you now must do:

1. Focus on the point of the ball.

2. Get a feel as to where the sideline is without ever looking at it. The receiver who starts looking down to see the sideline or the position of his feet will not catch a football because he will not see it hit his hands.

3. Concentrate on catching the ball without either foot touching the line.

Practice it frequently because there are a lot of balls caught at the sidelines, and unless that "feel" is part of a skill to be used in a game, then the receiver won't be very good at it. In high school and college football, only one foot needs to be in bounds. But in this drill, make sure that both feet stay on the playing field, because a receiver can often lapse into a false sense of security that one of his feet is certain to stay in bounds. Not really! The drill can be run first at slow motion, so the player can begin to get that "feel" of the sideline and keeping his feet in bounds, and then the tempo can be revved up but always

FIGURE 10-17

FIGURE 10-18

FIGURE 10-19

FIGURE 10-20

FIGURE 10-21   **FIGURE 10-22**

BAD BALL DRILL (Low Throw): Coach Coslet sets himself to throw a low ball to J.J. as he comes out of his break and accelerates across the middle (10-21 & 10-22). As the ball arrives below his knees he focuses on the "black spot," (10-23) reaches down to catch the ball (10-24), bringing it under control in his body, (10-25) and turns downfield (10-26).

with the aim of both catching the ball, putting it away and keeping those feet in the field of play.

Bad Ball Drill

This comes in three parts as receivers run back and forth across the field as if they were running the top end of a deep crossing pattern where the ball can come in high, low or behind them. There is no sense just catching easy tosses all the time because it won't always happen in a game. We've seen balls flop through the air like knucklers. Sometimes balls come well behind; the receiver misreads the defense, yet the quarterback throws to an open area in the zone, and the receiver has to adjust to save what would have been a bad throw. Anything a coach can think of to make the ball come in funny is good—end over end or even bounce it off the ground—just to make the receiver concentrate on the ball when it comes to him in a strange way. Here are three basic ways to throw it. In each instance, the receiver should run down the field and break to the inside.

FIGURE 10-23

FIGURE 10-25

FIGURE 10-24

FIGURE 10-26

FIGURE 10-27   **FIGURE 10-28**

BAD BALL DRILL (Behind Receiver): In a side view, Coach Coslet sees the ball about to arrive behind him, and begins to de-accelerate his speed and turn his shoulders (10-27 & 10-28) and then opens his hips to the ball as he comes around to make the catch (10-29). In a front view, he again de-accelerates his speed and turns his shoulders (10-30 & 10-31) before opening his hips to the ball and making the catch (10-32).

1. *High Throws.* The ball should be thrown far enough above the receiver's head to force him to get off his feet, or certainly stretch to a maximum height, to catch it. He must reach for it, either by leaping or stretching all-out, depending upon the ball's path, catch it, put in away under control, and then run. He should remember to stop the tip of the ball before it gets past his eyes so it will be easier to control.

2. *Low Throws.* The ball should be thrown below the knees. The receiver must catch it, control it to his body and keep running.

3. *Behind the Receiver.* As the receiver runs along a prescribed course, a ball is thrown in such a way that the receiver will have to deccelerate, open his hips to the ball and then make the catch. Above all else, he cannot simply reach backward with his arms because this will not open the hips and he will not be able to "give" with the ball. The result probably will be a dropped pass because he will not be in control of his body to make the catch.

FIGURE 10-29

FIGURE 10-30

FIGURE 10-31

FIGURE 10-32

FIGURE 10-33

The Wrong Way: The receiver reaches back for the ball without opening his hips (10-33). This does not allow him to "give" with the ball and will result in many dropped passes.

Drills for Passers and Receivers

Passers and receivers should work together as much as possible so all of their actions and reactions become so automatic that they will know without a word being said what the other will do. This can begin with a couple of good drills designed to help them survive difficult situations and perfect their techniques.

Wave-and-Scramble Drill

This is an asset to the quarterback because it will help his movement within the passing pocket. It will also help the receiver to move with the quarterback in situations where he must scramble out of the pocket and look for an open receiver. Receivers always must remember that whenever a quarterback gets into trouble and has to scramble, they should break off their patterns and come back to help him by running in the same direction as he does to give him a good target.

In this drill, the quarterback, a receiver and a coach or third player participate. The quarterback drops back for the pass. The third party stands behind the receiver and directs the quarterback either right or left. The receiver must change direction and move with the quarterback. The third party can signal at any time for the quarterback to

FIGURE 10-34

WAVE AND SCRAMBLE DRILL: Coach Coslet shows Ken, the quarterback, in which direction he should move (10-34 & 10-35) after he

FIGURE 10-35

FIGURE 10-36

drops back. When Ken is directed by a hand motion to reverse his route, Matt, the receiver, must do likewise and stay on that course (10-36) until Ken is directed to throw the ball (10-37).

FIGURE 10-37

FIGURE 10-38

PLAYING CATCH DRILL: *While just playing catch, Matt and J.J. simulate what they might do in a game. Matt, the quarterback, takes his stance over center with the ball (10-38) and leisurely takes a pass drop to get*

FIGURE 10-39

FIGURE 10-40

his feet moving and his mechanics in action (10-39). J.J. the receiver stations himself at various points to create a focused target (10-40 & 10-41) who has simulated just the last half step of the pattern, turning

FIGURE 10-42

FIGURE 10-41

his head to the passer, catching the ball and tucking it away before running a couple of steps (10-42 & 10-43).

FIGURE 10-43

throw the ball to the receiver who must be in control to catch it. Often, this drill can supplement the bad ball drill because the suddenness of the signal to throw may catch the receiver leaning the wrong way and having to stop and move his body in position to catch it.

The wave-and-scramble can also be a quarterbacks-only drill. In this version, the quarterback drops back and moves right or left at the command of the coach. Then he must shuffle up in the pocket, simulating an escape from the pass rush, and begin to move in an opposite direction, until he is given a signal to either change direction or throw the ball to the coach. At all times, he must keep the ball in proper throwing position because he may suddenly get a signal to stop and throw the ball and must get off a good throw.

Playing Catch Drill

This is not only a great way to enliven a game of catch but it also allows the receiver to catch more balls (that is great!), and it allows the quarterback to get warm and practice his throwing motion. They should always simulate what they do in a game, because it really is a waste of time to idly toss the ball back and forth.

The *quarterback,* after taking his stance as if standing over center, can take a leisurely pass drop to get his feet going and to get into his drop-back mechanics. The *receiver* can stand at various points so the quarterback will have a focused target to help his throwing accuracy. The receiver can simulate just the last half step of a pattern or turn his head back to the quarterback, then catch and tuck the ball; then he can take one move, as if to make a defender miss, before tossing the ball back to the quarterback.

Neither passer nor receiver will improve without repetition. Take care to use every fundamental all the time, so they will become automatic reactions in a game—so automatic that neither player will even be aware of where and when they were perfected.

About the Authors

KEN ANDERSON

Ken Anderson led the Cincinnati Bengals to four playoffs, including Super Bowl XVI, during his sixteen years in the NFL. He had a remarkable career, coming from Division III Augustana (Illinois) College to be a starting quarterback for the Bengals in his rookie season. Ken was the NFL's top-rated passer four times and his 70.55 completion percentage in 1982 is the best in NFL history. He also set the league record with 20 consecutive completions in one game, and he was named to three Pro Bowl teams. Ken is ranked among the all-time top ten NFL passers, gaining 32,834 yards, with 197 touchdown passes.

BRUCE COSLET

Bruce Coslet has been one of the NFL's brightest and most imaginative offensive coordinators since 1986, when he began working for the Cincinnati Bengals. In 1988, the AFC champions were ranked first in total yardage and were en route to Super Bowl XXIII. Bruce was also the team's receivers coach from 1981–85, where he directed the passing game and helped to develop such top-flight NFL receivers as Cris Collinsworth, Eddie Brown, Tim McGee and Rodney Holman. Bruce also was a tight end for the Bengals from 1969–76 (64 catches for 877 yards).

JACK CLARY

Freelance writer Jack Clary has co-authored, written and edited more than two dozen books on a variety of sports subjects during some 30 years as a journalist. These include a trivia book on the Minnesota Twins, and another, *So You Think You're a Baseball Fan* He also authored books with a NFL Hall of Famers Paul Brown (*PB*); Andy Robustelli (*Once a Giant, Always...*) as well as with former Orioles pitcher and television broadcaster Jim Palmer (*Jim Palmer's Way to Fitness*); former Bengals quarterback Ken Anderson (*The Art of Quarterbacking*). Some other books include *Great Moments in*

Pro Football, Careers in Sports, Army vs. Navy and The Game-makers with such renowned coaches as Tom Landry, John Madden, Chuck Noll, Don Shula and others. In addition to working as a consultant in all aspects of sports communications and marketing for his firm, Sports Media Enterprise, Clary spent 17 years as a sportswriter and columnist for The Associated Press, New York World Telegram & Sun and the Boston Herald Traveler.

Credits

Book Production/Design: Mountain Lion, Inc.
Cover Design: Michael Bruner
Copyediting: Deborah Crisfield
Photographs: Michael Plunkett and
Denny Landwehr/Corporate Photo Group
Typesetting: Elizabeth Typesetting Company
Mechanical: Production Graphics
Cover Photograph © Larry French